NINJA

NINJA

The True Story of Japan's Secret Warrior Cult

STEPHEN TURNBULL
Foreword by Dr Masaaki Hatsumi

Firebird Books

for Ian Clark

First published in the United Kingdom in 1991 by Firebird Books
P.O. Box 327, Poole, Dorset BH15 2RG

Copyright © 1991 Firebird Books Ltd
Text copyright © 1991 Stephen Turnbull

Distributed in the United States by
Sterling Publishing Co, Inc
387 Park Avenue South, New York, N.Y. 10016–8810

Distributed in Australia by
Capricorn Link (Australia) Pty Ltd
P.O. Box 665, Lane Cove, NSW 2066

British Library Cataloguing in Publication Data
Turnbull, S.R. (Stephen Richard), *1948–*
Ninja – the true story of Japan's secret warrior
cult.
1. Ninja
I. Title
356.167

ISBN 1 85314 109 7

Designed by Kathryn S.A. Booth
Typeset by Inforum Typesetting, Portsmouth
Monochrome origination by Castle Graphics, Frome
Colour separations by Kingfisher Facsimile
Colour printed by Barwell Colour Print Ltd. (Midsomer Norton)
Printed and bound in Great Britain by The Bath Press

CONTENTS

The author with Dr Hatsumi
This photograph was taken during Dr Hatsumi's visit to London in August 1988.

FOREWORD

by Dr Masaaki Hatsumi

The opening of my second seminar in London gave me a valuable opportunity for reflection. Since the Meiji Period, Japan has learned much from England, and continues to do so.

While in London I had the opportunity of meeting Stephen Turnbull, and was most impressed at the depth of his knowledge and the excellence of his research into Japanese history. I feel very strongly that the Japanese people should look more deeply into their country's history than they have been accustomed to do – and here in Stephen Turnbull we have a man who knows more about Japan than most Japanese.

My teacher Takamatsu-*sensei* always said: 'We should study our history very carefully, and not just rely on being told the facts by others'. I think this applies equally as well to ninjutsu as it does to all other studies of the samurai.

Stephen Turnbull's work is of the greatest importance in understanding the truth about ninja and ninjutsu, and it shows me that, even in this, Japan can learn from the West. I am delighted to have been asked to contribute this short Foreword to a book which will undoubtedly become the standard work on the subject for many years to come.

INTRODUCTION

There is no greater indication of the familiarity of a concept than that the word express-ing it enters a foreign language with no need for translation. During the last 50 or so years, Japan has furnished the English language with several such words, nearly all of which have military connections; 'samurai', 'hara-kiri', 'kami-kaze' – and more recently 'shogun' are all examples. Now we have another to join them – 'ninja'.

The ninja represent the dark side of the world of the samurai. In contrast to the image of the noble, fearless warrior, facing squarely on to his worthy opponent with drawn sword, the ninja is a creature of darkness and stealth, whose craft is guile, treachery and murder. The art of the overt warrior is thus replaced by the arts of the covert; here the skills that are most prized are not death-defying charges or challenges to noble opponents and expert swordsmanship, but rather those of subterfuge and deception.

Thus, the history of the ninja is a vital part of the history of the samurai of Japan that many samurai may have preferred to have remained unwritten. In fact, much of it re-mained just so. Nevertheless, a surprising amount was indeed recorded, sometimes in pride, sometimes in disgust – and most commonly of all, with a shrugging acceptance that in the ways of men ideals of behaviour often need a little help from that which is considered less than perfect.

The history of the ninja encompasses guerrilla warfare, assassination, espionage, magic and mysticism. It is not therefore surprising that the ninja should have surpassed every other breed of Japanese fighting man by being transformed into a modern-day cult, in which the historical figure grows into a superman who walks on water and flies through the air. What is remarkable is that this tendency to grant magical and superhuman powers to the ninja is at least three centuries old. Records of exploits which lift ninja above ordinary human accomplishments date from the latter part of the sixteenth cen-tury, and the popular image of the 'man in black' can be found in book illustrations as early as the 1780s. Add to this an amalgam of hero-legends, esoteric religious practices, magic and invisibility, and you arrive at the 'super' samurai – the ninja of today. In this book I intend to show that the truth about the ninja is every bit as strange as the fiction, and often much more impressive. The fiction will however not be neglected, for many ninja stories have a foundation in truth.

Acknowledgements
Many people have helped me in gathering the extensive but elusive materials I have used in compiling this work. I am particularly grateful to Miss Sakae Edamatsu of the National Diet Library in Tokyo, Ms Nicole White of the National Library of Australia, the staff of

Kyoto University Library and Tokyo National Museum, Mr Heishichirō Okuse and the staff of the Ninja Museum in Iga-Ueno, Hamish Todd of the British Library, the staff of the Uesugi Shrine in Yonezawa, and Miss Kyoko Naitō of N.H.K. Publications. Mr Kazukata Ogino kindly obtained for me the detailed maps of the old Iga province which proved indispensable in deciphering the complicated troop movements of the Iga Rebellion of 1579–81. I thank Dr Patricia Gudgeon for her comments on the possible causes of death of Uesugi Kenshin. I also thank Dr Masaaki Hatsumi for allowing me to conduct an in-depth interview with him, and for then agreeing to provide a Foreword.

Picture research for this book has been more than usually difficult, and here the majority of people I wish to thank have asked to remain anonymous. They include fellow members of the British Association for Japanese Studies, the Japan Society, the To-ken Society and the Society for Japanese Arts and Crafts. I am very grateful for the helpful leads provided by Ellis Tinios, Jack Hillier, Yu-Ying Brown, Brian Hickman, Robert Schaap, Chris Uhlenbeck, John Duxbury, Kurt Goldzung, Peter King, James Shortt, Ian Bottomley, Sebastian Izzard, Jon de Jong, Basil Robinson, Bernard Haase, Hendrick Lühl, Gottfried Reutz, Paul Ravicz, Philip Roach, John Cruikshank, Deborah Keeveny, Scott Johnson, Catherine Noden and Yoko Terashima. They joined in enthusiastically in what became known as my 'ninja hunt' and have helped me achieve what appeared once to be impossible: to illustrate a book about 'invisible men'.

Above all I wish to thank my dear wife Jo and my children Alex, Richard and Katy, without whom nothing would be possible.

Stephen Turnbull

Note

The techniques, skills, martial arts, potions and exploits of the ninja are detailed in this book entirely as a matter of historical and cultural record. The author and the publisher draw the attention of readers to the potential risks and dangers in the practice of all martial arts and associated activities, with their joint recommendation that these are studied or pursued only with expert advice and under legitimately qualified instruction and supervision.

Extracts from *No Surrender* by Hiroo Onoda are included by kind permission of André Deutsch Ltd. and extracts from *You Only Live Twice* by Ian Fleming by kind permission of Jonathan Cape Ltd.

1 THE FIRST NINJA

The image of the ninja as a black-clad, mysterious, super-samurai who is a deadly assassin and spy, is the popular concept which the word brings to mind today, and all these
elements have some basis in reality. For the purpose of definition I shall take the view
that the study of the ninja is the legitimate study of all aspects of unconventional Japanese warfare, from intelligence gathering to assassination, and from guerrilla warfare to
night raiding, and in view of the large number of words used for the practitioners of such
operations, I shall use the term 'ninja' except where the context is inappropriate. Two
closely related themes will be followed through this narrative: the development of the
popular 'superman' image of the ninja, and the strange way in which the arts of the ninja
turn traditional samurai values on their heads.

We begin with a brief look at these traditional values. The samurai were the military
class of Japan. They had begun as the followers of powerful, usually aristocratic, landowners in about the tenth century AD and, by the end of the twelfth century, had rele-
gated the Emperor of Japan, and his Chinese-inspired court, to a secondary position in
the government of the country. Instead, there was a military dictator, the *shōgun*, who
was the apex of a complex hierarchy of feudal obligation. The authority of the *shōgun*
was, however, never completely unchallenged, and over four centuries Japan was rent by
innumerable civil wars between samurai armies whose members held two things in
common: a belief in an ideal of behaviour in war that was handed down from generation
to generation, and a fierce pride in what were seen as the values of the samurai class.

These values consisted, in brief, of an image of a noble warrior who was well bred, and
also well trained in the martial arts. In earlier times the samurai were mounted and
wielded bows. In later times they were dismounted and carried swords. They were loyal
to their lord, fearless in battle, and faced squarely on to their equal and worthy opponents
whom they challenged to single combat. So fiercely was this ideal held, in fact, that the
movement of thousands of troops and the bombardment from firearms that dominated
Japanese battlefields from the 1550s onward were seen merely as a preliminary stage to
the decisive encounter between these noble knights of Japan. Even on the occasions of
these huge conflicts there was still a particular glory to be obtained by being the first into
the fray. Victory was crowned by the taking of an enemy's head, but should a samurai
experience the disgrace of defeat, then the shame and dishonour could be wiped away by
the dramatic act of *seppuku* (popularly called *hara-kiri*), which was suicide by cutting
open one's abdomen.

There was no place in this quixotic dreamworld for a knife in the back, or the destruction of a fortress at dead of night by warriors who were never seen by their victims. Yet all

9

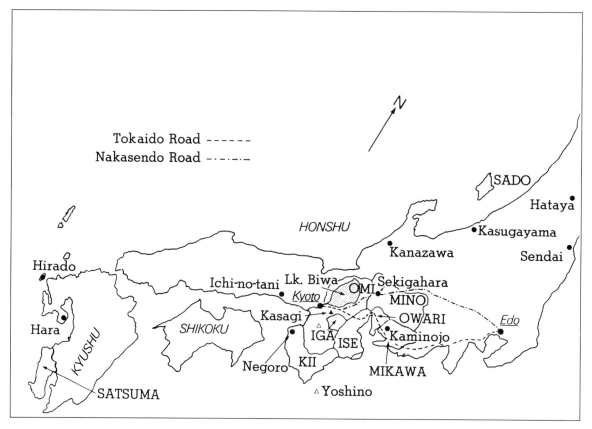

The Land of Japan
This map shows the overall layout of the Japanese islands, excluding Hokkaidō and the northern tip of Honshū. The historical provinces of central Japan which are mentioned in the text are indicated, as are the principal lines of communication.

these things happened and were vitally necessary for success. This was the dark side of the samurai tradition, the world of the warriors called ninja, who delivered victory by a process that reversed all that the samurai ideals stood for. Ninja did not face squarely on to their opponents, nor did they allow them the opportunity of a challenge. In sharp contrast to the fierce loyalty of the samurai ideal, the ninja represent the sole example of the use of paid mercenaries in samurai history, and there was also no particular honour attached to being the first into the battle. If it could be done with an assassin's knife in hand, preferably before the battle had even begun, then it was no more than an inglorious aid to victory.

Who Were the Ninja?

The expression *ninja*, when written using *kanji*, the Chinese characters in which much of the Japanese language is written, is pronounced in the Chinese style, and consists of two separate ideograms: *nin* (in Japanese, with the addition of a phonetic ending, *shinobi*), and *sha* (in Japanese *mono*, meaning a person). The first character can have various meanings on its own depending upon the phonetic inflection, but all are to do with concealment and hiding.

10

When *nin-ja* is written with the insertion of the phonetic character *bi* between the two characters, the compound must be read with the Japanese locution *shinobi-mono*, or with the additional phonetic character *no- shinobi-no-mono*. Either may be shortened to *shinobi*, which is the word most usually found in pre-modern literature about the subject, including war-chronicles, diaries and plays. However, this is not a hard-and-fast rule, because many of the best authenticated descriptions of ninja activities do not in fact use either *shinobi* or *ninja*, even though it is clear from the context that these names would be appropriate. There is, instead, a long list of alternative expressions, examples of which can be found in the pages which follow, such as the use of the terms *rappa* and *kusa* in the *Hōjō Godai-ki*[1], and *kagimono-hiki* in the *Kōyō Gunkan*, the chronicle of the Takeda family.[2] The latter expression is a particularly apt one as its literal meaning is 'sniffing and listening'! Alternatively, they can be referred to in terms of the actual uses of which *shinobi* were put, as *kanchō* (spies) or *teisatsu* (scouts).

Almost as familiar as ninja in English form is the expression *ninjutsu*. This is the all-embracing term most often used for the corpus of ninja knowledge and skills, *jutsu* being the same suffix meaning 'technique' that appears in *kenjutsu* (swordsmanship) and *jūjutsu* (the techniques of grappling). *Shinobi-no-jutsu* is quite common as an alternative.

The Japanese use of a word such as *ninja* for the practitioners of undercover operations, however, suggests more than just the employment of a convenient collective noun. It implies the existence of an élite group, a hereditary caste, or a secret brotherhood

Traditional samurai values – the Battle of Shijō-Nawate
The world of the ninja held a mirror up to the traditional values of the samurai class, and this triptych by Yoshitoshi (about 1862) illustrates these ideals of behaviour in no uncertain terms. It depicts one of the most gloriously heroic and doomed episodes in samurai history: the last stand of the three surviving leaders of the Kusunoki family at the Battle of Shijō-Nawate in 1348. Defeated and surrounded, the Kusunoki faced a hail of arrows as the enemy swept in to crush them, and met their death by hand-to-hand combat or seppuku. *Yoshitoshi has made the most of the heroic opportunities offered by this inspiring subject, and has produced a vivid picture very similar to the better known interpretation by Kuniyoshi, of whom Yoshitoshi was a pupil. See also Turnbull,* The Samurai – A Military History, *p. 104. (Courtesy of Christie's, London.)*

of initiates rather than simply the existence of a set of techniques performed by a loosely defined set of individuals, such as footsoldiers sent on spying missions or local farmers hired for reconnaissance. This view of ninja as the members of a closed, cabalistic society whose deadly techniques were passed down from master to chosen initiate is the essence of what may be termed the 'modern myth' of the ninja cult, which we will study in more detail later in this book.

The Ninja's Chinese Ancestors

The ninja have a very long history indeed, with their origins to be found in Ancient China, an inheritance that was well-recognised in Medieval Japan. The first ever written recognition of the existence and importance of undercover warfare is contained in *The Art of War* by the Chinese Sun Tzu,[3] who lived sometime between the sixth and fourth century BC. *The Art of War* is the first great military classic, and has exerted an influence on martial thinking ever since. Fundamental to it is the notion that an army should only attack when the enemy has been made vulnerable from within. This process involves intrigue, rumour and intelligence-gathering. Sun Tzu's account of the use of spies, in which he sketches out much of what was to become recognised as ninja-lore, forms the thirteenth chapter of his work. After a brief introduction he expounds his theory that what divides the enlightened prince and the wise general from ordinary men is the possession of foreknowledge, and that this foreknowledge cannot be elucidated from divination or spirits, but only from men who have made themselves familiar with the actual enemy situation, in other words, secret agents.

The character Sun Tzu uses for spy in the title of the chapter is *kan*, which has the meaning of 'the space between two objects', or 'discord', an obvious reference to the ability of secret agents to cause division between allies. The same character is the first in the compound mentioned on page 11: *kanchō*, for spy (and the less familiar *kanja*, with the same ending as *nin-ja*). He goes on to distinguish five different types of *kan*, and it is interesting to note that this section is quoted word for word in a Japanese chronicle of 1684 entitled *Buyō Benryaku*, thus showing the extent of the dissemination of Sun Tzu's work. The *Buyō Benryaku* account begins with a definition of ninja: 'Ninja were those who lurked in their own and other provinces. Certain among them knew secret things and slipped into secure enemy castles. . . .'[4]

The author then goes on to equate contemporary ninja practice with Sun Tzu's five *kan*. In the Japanese reading they are *inkan, naikan, yūkan, shikan* and *shōkan*:

Inkan (native agents) refers to the employment by one's own side of inhabitants, usually villagers, of an enemy's province or country. As they cannot be properly trained, nor expected to take risks, their usefulness is limited to discovering the enemy's approximate dispositions.

Naikan (inside agents) are the officials of an enemy government whom one's own side takes into its pay. There are many reasons why such people may be tempted to betray their own masters, such as having been passed over for high office, or having failed to obtain a responsible position. There are others whose sole desire is to take advantage of the conditions warfare has brought about. Such men, writes Sun Tzu, may be approached, and afterwards rewarded liberally. They are the perfect *kan* in the sense of those who create discord, and the information they supply will be of much greater use than that obtained from a mere villager.

Yūkan literally means 'friendly agents', but the context explains that the understanding is of them being

Sun Tzu drills the concubines
According to the biography of Sun Tzu (discussed in Griffith's translation of Sun Tzu's Art of War*), the author of this, the first great military classic, was invited to demonstrate drill in front of the King of Wu, using the King's concubines as troops. They were at first inclined to giggle, until Sun Tzu showed them he was in earnest by ordering the beheading of the two concubines whom he had appointed as commanders of the right and left ranks. (From an early woodblock-printed edition of the* Taiheiki, *with illustrations by an unknown artist; Genroku 11 [1698]; private collection.)*

double agents. They are enemy agents whom we discover spying against us. We pardon them, bribe them and use them in the straightforward modern sense of a double agent.

Shikan (agents of death) is the chilling title for those of one's own agents who are regarded as expendable. They are deliberately given false information and sent on their way. When captured by the enemy the false information is disclosed, and the enemy commander adjusts his plans accordingly. The expendable nature of the *shikan* is explained by the fact that such an agent may well be discovered and put to death, but the false information will already have done its work. The commentary on Sun Tzu[5] gives as an example the case of a condemned man who was pardoned in order to use him as a *shikan*. He was disguised as a monk and made to swallow a ball of wax in which was concealed a fabricated letter to a very senior general in the enemy army. When the monk was apprehended he told his captors about the ball of wax, and as nature took its course the enemy acquired the letter, which incriminated the high-ranking general by suggesting collusion. The unfortunate and innocent general was immediately put to death, thus robbing the enemy of one of their ablest commanders. The 'expendable' monk soon followed him.

Shōkan (living agents) are the classic ninja-like spies, who go into enemy territory and return with valuable information. For this purpose men are selected who are pre-eminent in intelligence and hardiness. They are agile, brave and knowledgable. They have the ability to withstand great hardship, while also being able to gain access to those of the enemy who are closest to the seat of power. It is no wonder that Sun Tzu places such agents on the highest of pedestals. None but he should be closest to the commander, and none should be rewarded so generously.

As noted above, the chapter on spies is fundamental to Sun Tzu's philosophy. Warfare, in the conventional sense of the clash of armies on the battlefield, was viewed almost as a last resort. Such warfare was preceded by measures designed to weaken the enemy and cripple him from within. Thus the skilful commander used his spies to create division between brother generals and between allies. Information was constantly being gathered, while rumours were planted in its place. Deliberate attempts were also made to demoralise the enemy, until one arrived at the stage when the enemy was already defeated in spirit. At that point, and not before, the wise general launched his 'conventional' attack. Even then, though, the process of war was governed by restraint and thoughtfulness, because victory must be gained in the shortest possible time, with the minimum of casualties to one's own side, and with the minimum of avoidable damage to the enemy. There was no point in the needless wasting of enemy countries and the destruction of his cities. The clue to success in all of this was national unity. Preserve your own unity, and destroy that of your enemy – before war begins. The thirteenth chapter, therefore, may lay out the means for acquiring military intelligence, but its actual use permeates the whole of *The Art of War*. To Sun Tzu, warfare is honestly and unashamedly based on the deception of the enemy.

There are many instances in Japanese history where a chronicler refers to Sun Tzu and his 'tips for a good general'. On certain occasions a Japanese general recognises a particular feature on the battlefield and relates it to a hint or a warning by Sonshi, as Sun Tzu is known in Japanese. A well-known example is that of Minamoto Yoshiie (1041–1108) on his way to lay siege to the fortress of Kanezawa, who observed a flock of wild birds rising in disordered flight from a forest. He concluded, correctly, that an ambush had been laid, a lesson he had noted from Sun Tzu's treatise.[6] Many other instances can be quoted, evidence of how thoroughly the teaching of Sun Tzu had permeated the Japanese military hierarchy by the Middle Ages.

One may therefore perhaps be permitted to ask why, if Sun Tzu was so well known, were his precepts about slowly destroying from within and minimising casualties followed so infrequently? The whole trend of Japanese warfare, as we shall see in the chapters which follow, was the complete antithesis of restraint. Perhaps a clue lies in the writings of an earlier Western commentator on Japanese history. In Sir James Murdoch's lavish and often ludicrously moralising *History of Japan* there is a particularly caustic reference to the Chinese ancestry of the darker side of Japanese warfare. Murdoch is describing the time of the ninja heyday in Japan, which was the century and a half of interminable civil war between about AD 1450 and 1615 which historians refer to as the *sengoku-jidai*, the Age of the Country at War. The authority of the *shōgun* had all but collapsed, and a number of petty dictators called *daimyō* fought one another for as much territory as they could maintain. As great armies moved ponderously and conspicuously across the rice fields, bands of *shinobi* slipped unobtrusively into enemy castles to set fire to them or murder their keepers, or stole into an army's camp under cover of darkness to cause havoc and confusion. The principles behind such activities were well known to all the *daimyō* who used them. For the sake of their own survival they had to be fully acquainted with the range of techniques they could employ, and what could be brought into use against them.

Murdoch devotes several paragraphs to a denunciation of what he sees as the 'naked and full-bodied depravity of the old Chinese lore on espionage', as practised by the

Japanese warlords; the classic work of Chinese lore he attacks is Sun Tzu's *Art of War*:

Sometimes too the fortunes of a great house depended upon the astuteness of some exceptionally able retainer; and in such a case the baseness of the trickery and fraud to which hostile clans would resort to bring this retainer under his lord's suspicion, and so effect his fall and the subsequent ruin of the house whose main support he was, makes one blush for human nature.

The country was now in an interminable turmoil of war; but by 'war' a great deal more was meant than the mere ordering of campaigns and the handling of troops on the battlefield. It was 'war' conducted on the principles expounded in such Chinese manuals as Sonshi's. These works were now in the hands of nearly every one of the few that could peruse them; at night a professor – sometimes a Chinaman – would be set to read them aloud to the samurai gathered in the castle hall to hear him. In these Chinese analogues of Jomini and Clausewitz, what was chiefly expounded was not so much the principles of war as the dirtiest forms of statecraft with its unspeakable depths of duplicity. The most cynical, the very worst passages in the notorious Eighteenth Chapter of 'The Prince', pale before the naked and full-bodied depravity of the old Chinese lore on espionage. Sonshi's section on spies is truly abominable and revolting; yet this special section must be carefully conned by anyone who wishes to understand the fashion in which 'war' was waged in Japan at this time. In most respects the standard of public morality in the Empire was perhaps lower than it was in contemporary Italy, the only marked difference in favour of Japan being the comparative rarity, if not total absence, of cases of poisoning.[7]

Note how Murdoch compares Sun Tzu to Niccoló Machiavelli, that other great advocate of methods conventionally regarded as underhand. Machiavelli's 'notorious Eighteenth Chapter' of *The Prince* [8] advises the successful ruler to give an outward appearance of being kind, compassionate, honest and devout, while being prepared to act in exactly the opposite way when necessary.

But what was it about the 'Chinese lore on espionage' that so offended Murdoch? Perhaps the answer is that such an approach to conflict is totally in contrast to the other aspect of warfare so cherished by men: that the purpose of war is not merely victory but glorious victory. This was after all the samurai ideal, and it is merely one example of the way in which the ideal of the overt warrior conflicts with the arts of the covert. It also conflicts with the traditional Western view, expounded so neatly by the Duke of Wellington, that victory goes to the side that 'pounds hardest'. This philosophy, which would have been understandable to Murdoch, was to lead straight to the trenches of World War I and the concept of total war, which has its most ghastly expression in the bombing of civilians. A generation brought up under the shadow of nuclear warfare might look more kindly upon Sun Tzu, and see the 'knife in the dark' which so outraged Murdoch as a considerable blessing. Nevertheless, Murdoch's statement reminds us of the point I made earlier; that the arts of the ninja turned samurai values on their heads.

The Ninja come to Japan

According to Japanese tradition Sun Tzu's *Art of War*, and with it the concept of military intelligence, was introduced to Japan by Kibi Makibi (AD 693–775), who visited China twice in the position of ambassador, and brought back several classical texts, among which was the *Sonshi*. The *Shoku Nihongi*, compiled about AD 747 contains several quotations from *The Art of War*.

However, it is interesting to note that an earlier Japanese work, in fact the earliest Japanese book of all, was presented to the Court in AD 714, and contains a vivid account of an assassination in a style that would later be identified with ninja. The book is the *Kojiki*, the *Record of Ancient Events*, and the proto-ninja is Prince Yamato, son of the

Emperor Keiko. The legends of Prince Yamato are probably those of a composite character, but are none the less popular, summarising as they do all the qualities of the traditional lone Japanese warrior. The ninja incident which follows shows us quite clearly that such a paragon was not above using the arts of the covert warrior when it suited his purpose.

The *Kojiki* relates how Prince Yamato was banished by his father (he had murdered his brother for the crime of being late for dinner) and was ordered to put his energies to some use by quelling rebellious chieftains on the great southern island of Kyūshū. The rebels are referred to as *kumaso*, an alternative word to the more common *emishi* for the aboriginal inhabitants of the Japanese islands. When Yamato arrived at the *kumaso* headquarters he discovered that a party was in preparation in celebration of the completion of the building of the chief's dwelling. When the merrymaking began Yamato let down his long hair and combed it over his shoulders, then dressed himself in a robe and skirt obtained, along with a sword, from his aunt, the chief priestess of the Great Shrine of Ise. Thus disguised as a girl he joined in the celebrations. The two *kumaso* chieftains were attracted by the newcomer, and invited 'her' to sit between them. (An alternative version of the story mentions only one chieftain.) When the festivities are at their height Yamato pulled the sword from his robe and stabbed the elder of the brothers. The younger fled from the room in terror. Yamato pursued him and thrust his sword up his backside, but before being killed the younger brother asked the stranger to disclose his true identity, at which he granted Yamato the appellation *Yamato-dakeru* (Yamato the brave) in admiration for his exploit.[9]

Note the vital point played in the story by disguise, a means of deception that was to be found in many ninja stories in the centuries to come. A similar action under the cover of disguise appears in another old Japanese legend: that of General Raikō and the ogre of Ōeyama.

The Ōeyama monster was a demonic youth called Shutendōji (literally the 'wine-drinking youth'). Wine made him into a demon that could assume many forms, and he was wont to steal into Kyōto and take away sons and daughters to his fastness in the mountains. The commission to destroy him fell upon a hero called Raikō (the historical Minamoto Yorimitsu 944–1021), who chose four companions, Watanabe Tsuna, Urabe Suekata, Usui Sadamitsu and Sakata Kintoki to accompany him on the dangerous journey. The disguise they adopted was that of *yamabushi*, the wandering mountain monks who were later to be associated with the ninja. This disguise also gave them the opportunity to conceal their weapons and armour within the large climbing packs traditionally carried by the *yamabushi* on their pilgrimages. On their way they were presented with a jar of magic saké which they were urged to persuade the ogre to drink in order to paralyse him and leave him easy prey for their swords.

The venture went according to plan. Raikō and his men were invited into the ogre's palace and called to join in his feast, where Shutendōji, in his human form of a handsome youth, held state. The magical saké had the desired effect, and presently the chief of the ogres and his monstrous companions had all fallen asleep. Raikō and his men changed into their armour and attacked, at which point Shutendōji assumed his demonic form. With a mighty sweep of his sword Raikō took off the ogre's head, which shot up into the air with smoke and fire billowing from its nostrils. The severed head came down on top

Prince Yamato as a ninja
The Kojiki, *presented to the Japanese Court in AD 714, contains an account of the legendary Prince Yamato and his use of* ninjutsu. *Yamato disguised himself as a girl in order to win the confidence of two rebel chieftains, then slew them both with his concealed dagger during a feast. (From the print series* One Hundred Aspects of the Moon *by Yoshitoshi [1886]; private collection.)*

of Raikō, burying its fangs into his helmet. The dead body of the ogre, still writhing, was cut to pieces by Raikō's companions.[10]

This story is interesting on several levels. There is the use of disguise, particularly that of a *yamabushi*, which was to become a popular guise for secret agents and fugitives in the years to come. There is also the image of Shutendōji and his gang. Perhaps the basis of the story is that of gangs of robbers based in the mountains round Kyōto who preyed on travellers? (See Chapter 3 concerning the prevalence of bandits in the mountains of Iga province, legendary home of the ninja.)

Ninjutsu in the War Chronicles

Apart from such legends ninja-like activities may be found in the earliest of the genre known as *gunkimono* or *gunki-monogatari*, the 'war-tales' of the samurai. These epics, analogous to the *Iliad*, record the supposed deeds of the samurai heroes of the civil wars of the eleventh and twelfth centuries. Though sometimes questionable as a historical record, the *gunkimono* are very useful for the light they shed on samurai values and techniques of combat. The first of the *gunkimono* is the *Shōmonki*, which deals with the suppression of the rebel Taira Masakado, and was probably completed shortly after his death in AD 940.[11]

The *Shōmonki* includes a section which involves the use of a secret agent. He is employed in the fashion of Sun Tzu's *naikan* (inside agents), but the context makes it clear that he is to be regarded as an expendable *shikan* if it is necessary. The spy's employer is Taira Yoshikane, the Vice-Governor of Shimōsa Province and Masakado's uncle, who has vowed to bring his rebellion to an end. The *naikan* himself is Masakado's servant Hasetsukabe no Koharumaru.

Yoshikane seems to have made contact with Koharumaru and summoned him to his quarters. There he asked him to return to Masakado and spy on his master on Yoshikane's behalf. Yoshikane promised him lavish rewards and promotion in Yoshikane's army once the task was completed. Koharumaru swallowed the bait completely, and with a companion supplied by Yoshikane returned to Masakado's service. Each carried a load of charcoal, presumably to give some reason for Koharumaru's absence. During the two days he spent there on nightwatch Koharumaru took the man round the place and showed him the location of the storehouses. He also pointed out Masakado's sleeping quarters, and explained the general defensive layout. The man then returned to Yoshikane's headquarters leaving Koharumaru behind, and gave a full report of what he had found to Yoshikane, who soon launched a night attack. Yet in spite of his inside knowledge he was not victorious. Masakado's army resisted so tenaciously that 40 of the attacking army were killed. A worse fate was in store for the treacherous Koharumaru. Somehow, his misdeeds were found out, and he was captured and put to death in the manner of spies throughout history.

Secret Operations in the Gempei War

The samurai clans grew rich and powerful by suppressing rebellions against the throne such as that of Masakado. Eventually two clans in particular, the Minamoto and the Taira (of which Masakado had been a member) grew strong enough to be able to contest one another for supremacy, and the latter part of the twelfth century was dominated by the struggle between them, which, after sporadic fighting, developed into a protracted civil war known as the Gempei War, from the Chinese reading of the names of the Minamoto (*Gen*) and Taira (*Hei*). The story of the Gempei War is told within one of the greatest *gunkimono*, the *Heike Monogatari*. Being intended for an aristocratic audience who wished to hear of the deeds of their ancestors, undercover operations are not much in evidence. Nor for that matter are the deeds of the common footsoldiers, who outnumbered the élite mounted archers by twenty to one. Instead there are long descriptions of individual combat between overt warriors, noble, equal and accomplished, but quite late on in the narrative we come across a simple example of the sort of large-scale deception

The exploits of two comrades *(left)* and the Kawara brothers at Ichi-no-tani *(right)*
As a result of the traditional samurai obsession with being the first into battle, two warriors, Kumagai Naozane and Hirayama Sueshige, detached themselves from the main body which was preparing to make a dawn assault upon the Taira fortress of Ichi-no-tani in 1184. They delivered a night attack, which was a far cry from a 'ninja raid'. It was carried out mounted and to the accompaniment of a shouted challenge, but was none the less successful in its primary aim of individual glory. Meantime, two other samurai also made a very unconventional attack on Ichi-no-tani. Abandoning their horses, they scaled the walls under cover of darkness. No sooner were they within the compound than they bellowed out a challenge to individual combat. (From Vol. 9 of an early woodblock-printed edition of Heike Monogatari, *in 12 volumes, illustrated by an unknown artist; Meireki 2 [1656]; private collection.)*

of which Sun Tzu would have approved. It is in the description of the Battle of Yokota ga hara in 1182 (*Heike Monogatari* Vol. 6, Chapter 13):

. . . the Genji of Shinano, by the stratagem of Inoue no kuro Mitsumori, divided two thousand of their men into seven parties, each bearing a red flag, the colour of the Heike, and when the warriors of Echigo saw these emerging over the rocks and out of the defiles they set up a shout of joy, thinking that many were for their side in this province also. But as the different bands approached, at a given signal the whole seven drew together into one, and throwing away their red banners, suddenly replaced them with white ones and advanced to the onset. When the men of Echigo saw this manoeuvre panic seized them and they cried out: 'Ah! We have been deceived!'[12]

Apart from this example of the use of deception, the only case of anything resembling a 'ninja attack' occurs as a result of one of the overt warrior's great obsessions: that of earning the glory of being the first into battle. There are few actions in samurai history that are not accompanied by keen rivalry to achieve this particular distinction, and if the object of attack was a fortified place the ninja skill of castle-entering could come in very useful. The Battle of Ichi-no-tani in 1184 is a case in point. The Taira were defending a stockade fort which opened on to the sea at Ichi-no-tani, now a little seaside town to the west of Kobe. To the north of the fortress were very steep cliffs, down which the famous general Yoshitsune was to lead a mounted detachment in the celebrated surprise attack which won the battle. But the night before the battle it appeared even to those on the attacking side that any assault over the cliff would be impossible, and those samurai desirous of glory, and in particular the supreme accolade of being the first into battle, realised that a more promising course of action would be to join the forces that were massing for the main attack along the beach. Kumagai Naozane was the first to move in this direction, but instead of joining his comrades in arms he passed them by and rode straight up to the walls of Ichi-no-tani where he called out his name to the defenders, hoping for a worthy challenge. None came, and Kumagai soon realised that he was not alone, but had been joined by a fellow samurai called Hirayama who had similar aspirations. The Taira eventually came out to fight them outside the walls until they were driven back inside, but not before Hirayama had entered the fortress and taken a head:

Kumagai had taken much spoil and had been the first to arrive before the entrance, but as the gate was shut he had been unable to enter, whereas Hirayama, who had come up later, charged within the gate when it was opened, so that it was difficult to decide who had the honour of being foremost.[13]

Their surprise attack, if such it can be called, had therefore taken place mounted, and to the accompaniment of an open challenge. While this was going on, however, two other Minamoto samurai in a different detachment were separately achieving distinction in a very unconventional way. It was unusual because the samurai of the Gempei Wars were regarded as élite mounted archers whose primary weapon was the bow, supplemented by the *tachi* (sword) and *tantō* (dagger). In Chapter 11 of Volume 9 of *Heike Monogatari* we read how two young brothers, Kawara Jirō and Kawara Tarō, abandoned their horses for a night raid. This may well be one of the earliest recorded, and is also interesting in that although they are behaving like ninja, they keep their bows as their main weapons. Note also the striking contrast with later, silent, ninja raids in that no sooner are they within the fortress than, like Kumagai above, they bellow out a challenge to worthy opponents!

. . . calling their retainers and bidding them bear the tidings of their end to their wives and children, they dismounted and put on straw sandals, and then carrying their bows only, they climbed over the barricade under cover of darkness. Standing within the stronghold, though the colour of their armour could not be distinguished in the starlight, they shouted loudly: 'Kawara Tarō Kisaichi Takanao and his brother Jirō Masanao, first in the attack on Ikuta-no-mori!'[14]

We may judge just how novel an event like this was from the reactions of the Taira samurai, who at first held back from attacking the intruders until Jirō and Tarō had made reaction inevitable by loosing volleys of arrows at them. After the initial confusion two archers of equal skill to the brothers replied in kind:

Coming forward he drew his bow to the arrowhead, and taking careful aim, let fly his shaft at Kawara-no-Tarō, who staggered forward pierced through the breastplate. As he tried to support his failing strength on his bow his brother Jirō ran up, and taking him on his back, made to climb the barricade once more, when Manabe, fitting a second arrow to his string, shot him under the skirts of his armour, so that both brothers fell dead together. His retainers then ran up and cut off both their heads, which they brought and showed to the commander, Shin-Chūnagon Tomonori. 'Ah, the pity of it', he said, 'that two such valiant men at arms should die. Would that their lives could have been spared, for they were each worth a thousand men.'[15]

Thus ended a unique episode in samurai history. Future night raids would never be conducted in such a gentlemanly fashion, nor would a castle commander speak in terms of praise of those who had thwarted his defences.

2 THE EMPEROR'S NINJA

The Gempei War ended in 1185 with the defeat of the Taira and the complete triumph of the Minamoto, whose leader, Minamoto Yoritomo, was appointed *shōgun* in Kamakura in 1192. The years between 1185 and 1189 were marred by the feud between Yoritomo and his talented brother Yoshitsune, whose military skill had gained the ascendancy the Minamoto now enjoyed. We will examine in Chapter 9 the ninja-like role of Yoshitsune and his followers on their flight from Yoritomo, and the popular myth of him forming a school of *ninjutsu* called the Yoshitsune-ryū.

From the time of Yoritomo onwards, the history of Japan is dominated no longer by the Emperor and court, but by the successive dynasties of shōgunal or regent families who fought for supremacy under the god-emperor. The destabilising effects of assassination and division, foreseen by Sun Tzu as vital to the conduct of warfare, continued to play their vital part. In 1193 a hunting party of Yoritomo was disturbed by an assassination as the two Soga brothers, Jūrō and Gorō, took their revenge on one of Yoritomo's favourites, who was the murderer of their father. The revenge of the Soga brothers, admittedly, is more of a classic of vengeance than deception, but the secrecy in which they plotted their revenge, reflected centuries later in the epic story of the *Forty-seven Rōnin*, makes it worthy of mention here. Nor was the Minamoto family spared the trauma of death at an unknown hand, because both the second and the third Minamoto *shōgun* were murdered. Sanetomo, who was the third and the last, met his end at the hands of an assassin in the New Year of 1219. He was attacked on the steps leading up to the Hachiman Shrine in Kamakura one snowy morning.[1]

The tumultuous events of the Mongol attempts at invasion of Japan in 1274 and 1281 were marked by incredible bravery, dogged determination and divine intervention in the form of the famous storm, the *kami-kaze*, that wrecked the invasion fleet. There seems to have been little use of covert operations by either side, apart from a little spying and some psychological warfare on the part of the Mongols, whose massacres on the islands of Iki and Tsushima were designed to intimidate the Japanese mainland. According to Yamada, the only authority for the story, the Mongols stripped their captives from Iki and nailed them by the palms of their hands to the prows of their ships.[2] One may perhaps assume that some intelligence was carried out on the mainland between the two invasions so that the Japanese could prepare, but clear examples of undercover warfare had to wait a full century, when a further series of civil wars unexpectedly provided the conditions whereby the arts of the covert warrior could flourish as never before.

These wars, the Nambokuchō Wars, (the name literally means the Wars of the Southern and Northern Courts), had their origin as an attempt by the Emperor Go-Daigo (reigned

1319–38) to overthrow the *bakufu*, or shogunate, and re-establish the imperial power to a state it had not known for many centuries. He was helped early on in his efforts by a samurai general called Kusunoki Masashige (1294–1336), whose use of unconventional and ninja-like tactics has led to him being credited with founding a school of *ninjutsu* called the Kusunoki-ryū. Under Masashige's leadership the Imperial cause prospered, but his death led not to an Imperial restoration, but only to a new *shōgun* from a branch of the Minamoto called the Ashikaga. The fighting still continued, and for a period of half a century there were two rival emperors: the Ashikaga nominee in the 'Northern Court' in the capital, Kyōto and Go-Daigo's successors who maintained their legitimacy from a 'Southern Court' in various secret locations in the mountains of Yoshino.

What is now regarded as Masashige's *ninjutsu* was in fact very skilful guerrilla warfare, marked by surprise attacks, night operations, and distinguished above all by Sun Tzu's insistence that warfare was the art of deception. The conditions which governed the conduct of the Nambokuchō Wars lent themselves particularly well to this mode of combat, and enable us to see for the first time in samurai history the successful operation of the art of the covert warrior. There is much besieging of fortified places in hilly and wooded country, and pitched battles are the exception rather than the rule. In fact Kusunoki Masashige was to meet his death at an ill-judged pitched battle at Minatogawa in 1336. The ill-judgement, incidentally, was that of Go-Daigo, and not Masashige, who went willingly to his death in obedience to the commands of his sovereign, an act that was posthumously to place Masashige on the highest pinnacle of samurai heroes. In the years before Minatogawa, pitched battles had been avoided at all costs. Both sides used undercover operations in the bitter fighting in the forests, though it is Masashige's stratagems that are better remembered.

The accounts of his campaigns are contained within one of the greatest of the *gunkimono*, part history, part romance, called the *Taiheiki*, much of which was compiled between about 1360 and 1380. Like the *Heike Monogatari*, it has to be treated with caution as a historical source, but it paints an excellent picture of the values held by samurai society at the time, and we can glean much from it that enriches our picture of unconventional forms of warfare in fourteenth-century Japan. It is full of references to the Chinese classics including Sun Tzu, and unlike the *Heike Monogatari* there is much in the *Taiheiki* that falls within the sphere of *ninjutsu*, for the very good reasons of strategy and topography mentioned above.

Night Raid on Kasagi

By far the most interesting undercover operations and irregular warfare during the Nambokuchō Wars are found in the pages dealing with the defence by Kusunoki Masashige and others of a series of fortified positions in the wooded mountains round about Yoshino. The first account however, shows the forces of the *bakufu* (shogunate) using a ninja-like raid against Masashige's side. This was carried out against the first stronghold held by the Imperialists which was Kasagiyama, a mountain overlooking the Kizugawa. (It was very close to the border with Iga province, the territory that during the next century was to become indelibly linked with the ninja.) The *bakufu* forces had already dislodged Go-Daigo's son Prince Morinaga – the Prince of the Great Pagoda – from his

Samurai climbing a castle's walls
Although the incident illustrated here is of much later date than the raid on Kasagi castle described in the Taiheiki, *the eagerness with which the samurai scale the castle walls shows the ready acceptance of such risks as part of the samurai tradition. (From* Ehon Taikō-ki, *a romance based on the life of Toyotomi Hideyoshi by Takenouchi Kakusai, and illustrated by Okada Gyokuzan; published in Ōsaka by Kobayashi Rokubei in Kyōwa 2 [1802]; private collection.)*

base on Mount Hiei, near Kyōto, where he led the famous 'warrior monks'. They now concentrated on Kasagi to deliver a devastating night raid.

According to the *Taiheiki* the decisive moment in the fate of Kasagi was the arrival on the scene of two *bakufu* samurai eager for glory: Suyama Tōzō Yoshitaka and Komiyama Jirō. They discussed between themselves the example of the exploits of Kumagai and Hirayama in entering the fray at Ichi-no-tani, but appreciated the fact that the fight for Kasagi had been going on somewhat too long for anyone to claim to be the first into battle. So the two heroes conceived of the idea of gaining even greater glory by entering the castle in secret under the cover of wind and rain, and leading a night attack:

They took two lead ropes for horses, a hundred feet long, knotted them together at intervals of a foot, and tied a grapnel at the end, that by hanging the ropes from branches and boulders they might climb over the rocks.

On that night one could see nothing, however much one looked, for it was the last night of the lunar month. Moreover it was a night of furious rain and wind, when opposing armies would not go forth to clash in battle. With swords and daggers on their backs, the fifty men began to climb at the northern ramparts of the castle, a rock wall fifteen hundred feet high, where even a bird could not fly easily. By various ways they went up for seven hundred and fifty feet, until with perplexed hearts they beheld rocks like folding screens, rising in layers above them in place of smooth green moss and ancient pines with drooping limbs.[3]

The reconnaissance they carried out after entering the castle was thorough and precise. They noted which areas were heavily defended, and from which provinces the various units had come. They also observed that the very steep northern side was hardly guarded at all. Suyama and Komiyama then set out to discover where Emperor Go-Daigo was based. They were challenged on the way, and responded by claiming that they were a special detachment ordered to guard against surprise night attacks. After this enounter they were able to walk around freely, and added to the illusion by ordering the defenders whom they met to be on special alert!

When Suyama and his men had beheld everything, even to the imperial abode, they made their hearts strong, bowed down in front of the god of the mountain, climbed to the peak above the Main Hall, lit a fire in a deserted compound, and raised a battle cry altogether.[4]

The *bakufu* forces at the foot of the mountain, who appear not to have been told about the raid for fear of spoiling the climbers' glory, concluded that deserters in the castle had started a fire, and prepared for an attack. Meanwhile Suyama and his 50 men, who were now familiar with the layout, dispersed to strategic points and set fire to towers, running around and making as much noise as possible. When the confusion was at its highest, and presumably both audible and visible from the valley below, the main *bakufu* army attacked. As the 'regular troops' poured in Emperor Go-Daigo fled in bare feet. He was later captured as he tried to join his son in Kusunoki Masashige's fortress at Akasaka.

It is fascinating to note how this raid on Kasagi, which led to this mountain fortress being abandoned for the duration of the war, has so many of the features we will recognise in all subsequent ninja night raids. There is the cover of darkness, the silent climb, a speedy reconnaissance, and then all hell breaks loose as buildings are fired. The most amusing point about it is, of course, that it was used against an ally of Kusunoki Masashige, rather than on his behalf, but from now on it is this loyal and intelligent fighter who dominates the scene.

The Prince and *Ninjutsu*

The *Taiheiki*'s account of the flight of Masashige's comrade in arms, Prince Morinaga 'of the Great Pagoda', adds an interesting anecdote about the magical side of *ninjutsu*, in the form of spells to make oneself invisible. (*Ninjutsu* is sometimes translated as 'the art of invisibility'.) Prince Morinaga was in any case a very accomplished young gentleman, and the *Taiheiki* tells us that he:

. . . vaulted over seven foot screens more nimbly than Chiang-tu, and in fencing mastered the precepts of Tzu-fang, nor did he fail to read completely even the shortest of the secret military treatises.[5]

In addition to the works of Sun Tzu he also had great faith in the power of magic. When Akasaka fell and both he and Masashige were forced to flee, Prince Morinaga made his way to the Hannya-ji in Nara. Here he stayed concealed and safe from pursuers, until one day he heard a number of horsemen ride up:

In the Buddha Hall he saw three great Chinese boxes with legs, containers of the *Daihannya Sutra*, left out where a monk had begun to read. The lids of two of them were closed, but more than half the sacred writings were taken out of the other one that stood open. The Prince laid himself down in that open box, pulled the sacred writings on top of him, and silently recited incantations to hide his person from the eyes of men.[6]

Magic spells to ensure invisibility are one of the skills attributed later to ninja. On this occasion they appear to have worked, because the samurai looked in all the boxes except the open one in which the Prince lay concealed. When they had gone, in an act owing more to commonsense than *ninjutsu* the Prince left the chest and climbed into one of the others that had already been examined. Sure enough the troops came back to search the

The Prince of the Great Pagoda

Prince Morinaga, the 'Prince of the Great Pagoda', was the son of Emperor Go-Daigo. He was well versed in the Chinese military classics and skilled in the martial arts. He was also adept at ninjutsu in the sense of the 'art of invisibility', as shown in the text where he uses incantations to prevent his enemies from discovering that he is concealed in a chest. (From an early woodblock-printed edition of the Taikeiki, *with illustrations by an unknown artist; Genroku 11 [1698]; private collection.)*

one they had omitted the first time, and the Prince survived to fight another day. He then left Nara disguised as a *yamabushi* pilgrim, and made his way to Kumano.

The Stratagems of Kusunoki

The *bakufu* forces then concentrated their attacks upon Kusunoki Masashige's final fortress – Chihaya, deep in the forests and built on a precipitous mountain. Chihaya still impresses one today, as do the well-known stories in the *Taiheiki* of Masashige's defences. The imperialists had obviously benefited from the experience at Kasagi, and most of the initiative seems to lie with the defenders. On one occasion a defender pretended to betray the castle, and the *bakufu* samurai who sallied in fell into a prepared pit.

A brave attempt by the *bakufu* to construct a bridge that could be swung across a chasm to the castle ended when Kusunoki's men set fire to it. Rocks and huge logs were arranged to fall upon attackers. Water was carefully conduited from roofs into storage vessels ready for a prolonged siege. Kusunoki Masashige also created a clever sort of deception early one morning:

With rubbish he made twenty or thirty figures of a man's stature, clad them up in helmets and armour, armed them with weapons, and set them up behind folding screens at the foot of the castle in the night. At the rear he stationed five hundred mighty men of valour, to raise a great battle shout when the dawn mists began to brighten.[7]

When the attackers gathered to assault the dummies Masashige let drop a load of rocks, which considerably mortified the pride of the *bakufu*, as well as causing injury.

It may be straining the definition of *ninjutsu* somewhat to give this label to Masashige's activities, but they certainly have enough respectability for him to be credited with forming his own school of *ninjutsu*, the Kusunoki-ryū. But, as noted earlier, Masashige's life ended on the battlefield of Minatogawa, where no tricks could save him. His son Masatsura continued the fight where Masashige had left off, and the Nambokuchō Wars dragged on for another 50 years, the Emperors of the Southern Court battling it out from their final strongholds in Yoshino. Even after 1392, when the Wars officially ended and succession was granted to the Northern Court, there were sporadic disturbances in the name of some 'Southern Emperor' or other, often carried out by a descendant of the Kusunoki family.

The Kyōto Raid

Despite claims that Masashige founded the Kusunoki-ryū, his campaigns and stratagems, and also the Kasagi Raid, were clearly carried out by regular soldiers acting in an irregular way. There is no evidence in any of the above accounts of anything like a ninja unit in the sense of a specialised force. The first record of such a unit, however, does occur in the *Taiheiki*, and is somewhat surprising in that it shows us that ninja were by no means infallible. The operation, which Yamaguchi claims is the first group action by *shinobi*, in fact suffered failure even before it was due to begin.[8]

Yamaguchi does not give a date for the operation, but it would appear to be sometime subsequent to the establishment of the Ashikaga Shogunate in 1338. Three loyalist conspirators were involved: Miyake Saburō Takatoki of Bizen province, Nitta Sa'emon-no-suke Yoshiharu and Hagino Hikoroku Tomotada of Tamba province. The last named did not even have time to join forces with his fellow conspirators, because he was attacked by the Yamana and forced to surrender. The other two withdrew from the Inland Sea provinces to Kyōto, and sent out an urgent letter requesting immediate reinforcements, which began arriving in dribs and drabs. Nitta was concerned that the assembly of such a great army would be easily detected, so he split it up into various units which were grouped in strategic positions around the city. These movements were, however, detected by the Lay Priest Tsugi, a *bakufu* official who bore the title of Kyōto Shōshidai.

Tsugi hurriedly gathered an army and launched an attack on the still fragmented army of Nitta. His decision about where to attack is interesting, because he moved first against a Kyōto mansion called the Shijōmibu where Miyake Tadatoki had concealed his band of *shinobi*. This is probably the first time that such a word appears in a chronicle to denote a distinct group of individuals, but Tsugi's realisation that they had to be defeated before all others shows that even at this stage the term *shinobi* had a very real meaning, and considerable implications. Fearsome though they may have been, these ninja were no guarantee of an easy victory. They appear to have been taken completely by surprise, a turn of events so unexpected that I checked my translation four times! Yamaguchi states that they fought back until they had no arrows left, then committed *hara-kiri*. Thus the loyalist plot collapsed, the greatest compliment to the skills of the ninja being that once they were defeated, then the whole army rapidly followed.

As additional evidence of ninja fallibility Sasama quotes an obscure chronicle called

The use of dummy troops
The ninjutsu of the Kusunoki-ryū of Kusunoki Masashige (1294–1336) was in reality no more than expert guerilla warfare, of which this incident is celebrated. He rigged up dummy troops from spare armour and straw, and enticed the enemy into attacking them. (From an early woodblock-printed edition of the Taiheiki, *with illustrations by an unknown artist; Genroku 11 [1698]; private collection.)*

the *Yoshōki*, which reads: 'In the Sixth Year of Jōji (1367), on the eleventh day of the sixth month, Tadaoka Rokurōza'emon shot down a *shinobi* who had entered Ototsu Castle'.[9]

The Kakitsu Affair

We conclude this chapter with a remarkable series of events that marked the final attempts to salvage the Southern Court's claim to legitimacy, brought about by a series of treacherous attacks. The affair began with the murder by the Akamatsu family of the *shōgun* Ashikaga Yoshinori in 1441. This was a particularly underhand affair, as the victim had been invited to a banquet at the home of Akamatsu Mitsusuke on the pretext of celebrating a recent victory. Dinner was followed by a performance of dancing, and as the *shōgun* sat engrossed in the entertainment a herd of horses suddenly broke into the garden. Their arrival, planned by the Akamatsu, caused sufficient panic and confusion for the *shōgun* to be set upon and murdered. That the Akamatsu were not alone in their plotting is shown by the fact that other samurai seemed very loathe to ride off and punish them, but eventually the *shōgun* was avenged, and the Akamatsu banished.

Two years later another incident occurred. At first it was totally unrelated to the murder, but the affairs soon got intertwined. Some dogged supporters of the Southern Court, including a member of the Kusunoki family, launched an attack on the Imperial

Palace and escaped with a number of items of the Crown Jewels, which ensured the legitimacy of the emperor. They made their way to the Yoshino mountains, where they maintained a newly founded Southern Court under a rival emperor until 1458. At this point the treacherous Akamatsu re-enter the story, for they realised that one way to restore their family's position would be to destroy the new pretenders to the throne. They did it in a manner that deserves the appellation of *ninjutsu*, though theirs was not a sudden raid. Instead they made the long journey through the mountains, and tricked their way into the confidence of the Southern Emperor. This part of the operation may not have been too difficult because it had been one of their family who had murdered the hated *shōgun*. They soon won the confidence of the loyalists, and then one dark night, under the cover of a heavy fall of snow, they killed the Emperor and recovered the jewels. There is a colourful legend that they buried the Emperor's head in the snow of the Obagamine Pass, meaning to recover it later, but blood seeped out of the neck and revealed its presence to their pursuers.

The simple story related above is told in several histories. It marked the final destruction of the Southern Court and the rehabilitation of the Akamatsu, and it is interesting to note that the current fascination with ninja has led to an increased emphasis on the ninja-like aspects of the raid. For example, a guide book to the area states simply that the attack on the Southern Emperor was carried out by six ninja, even though the word does not appear in the primary sources.

3 IGA AND KOGA

The events of the Nambokuchō Wars, described in Chapter 2, were fought out in an area of Japan not far distant from the two places indelibly associated in the popular mind with ninja and *ninjutsu*: the province of Iga and the southern area of Omi province known as Koga. We shall note in Chapter 4 that ninja and their activities were by no means confined to these two areas nor entirely dependent upon them, but the bulk of historical evidence suggests that the popular view of Iga and Koga as the most important cradle of ninja is broadly correct. In other words, the inhabitants of the Iga/Koga area, (the regions share a common border) developed a certain expertise in the skills and techniques that were to become known as *ninjutsu*, and, more importantly, these skills were both recognised and used by outsiders from quite an early time.

Region of Romance
A brief glance at a map of Medieval Japan gives one a clue as to why the Iga/Koga area could have the potential to produce a number of independent-minded families who by their military skills were sufficiently secure to be able to place these talents at the disposal of others. Iga province (now the northwestern part of Mie prefecture), was entirely landlocked, and almost the whole length of its borders followed the tops of several ranges of mountains. The villages in the flatlands within, therefore, nestled inside a ring of natural defences, pierced only by steep mountain passes. The one side of Iga that is not entirely protected by mountains is the north, where it borders on to its 'ninja neighbour' Koga, the southern portion of Omi province. It was a situation somewhat analogous, though on a much smaller scale, to that of contemporary Switzerland, whose mountains provided such a good natural defence that its equally formidable inhabitants could become the mercenary soldiers of Europe, with the Tokugawa *shōgun*'s Edo castle troops, recruited from Iga and Koga, equivalent to the Swiss Guards of the Vatican.

A more detailed look at the topography reveals that the region lies just to the south of the 'neck' of Medieval Japan, the narrow strip of land between Lake Biwa and the Bay of Owari that divides the country neatly in two. At the mouth of Lake Biwa lay the then capital, Kyōto, and through this corridor ran the two main highways to the East: the Tōkaidō which followed the Pacific coast, and the Nakasendō which turned inland and threaded through the vast mountains of the 'Japan Alps' to join the Tōkaidō in the vicinity of modern Tōkyō. The two roads were in fact one and the same (heading east from Kyōto) as far as Kusatsu. The Nakasendō then turned northeast along the edge of Lake Biwa, while the Tōkaidō headed for the sea on the coast of Ise province, just skirting north of Iga/Koga by the Suzuka Pass.

It was also an area which formed a bridge between the civilisation of the main trade routes to the capital, and the vast and wild mountains of the Kii Peninsula to the south, which amaze one even today by the solitude they present for a region so close to the urban sprawl of Ōsaka and Kyōto. Directly to the west of the Iga/Koga border lies Mount Kasagi, first refuge of the Southern Emperor. To the southwest lies Yoshino, his last hiding place, and beyond that the seemingly endless chain of mountains known at this time only to the villagers who lived their entire lives in one tiny valley, or to the wandering *yamabushi* who traversed this wild country on their pilgrimages. Several accounts refer to these mountains as the haunt of bandits who acted as highwaymen along the Tōkaidō and pirates on the sea coast of nearby Ise province. Many of the ninja myths, such as the legendary outlaw Ishikawa Goemon who was supposed to be adept in *ninjutsu*, no doubt have their origin in the elaboration of the exploits of very unmagical gangs of robbers.[1]

Iga and Koga therefore have all the ingredients for romance. But what historical foundation is there for the greatest romantic legend of all, that this was the homeland of the ninja?

The Ninja of Iga and the Ashikaga

The earliest written reference which associates ninja with Iga or Koga occurs in the supplement to the *Nochi Kagami*, the annals of the Muromachi *bakufu*. In one particular section, as quoted by Sugiyama, we read:

> Concerning ninja, they were said to be from Iga and Koga, and went freely into enemy castles in secret. They observed hidden things, and were taken as being allies. In the Western Lands (i.e. China) they were called *saisaku*. Strategists called them *kagimono-hiki*.[2]

The above description of their activities in 'enemy castles in secret' tallies well with many later accounts of castle attacks. The section goes on to mention a specific action in which Iga men were involved. Here we are instructed to read *shinobi* rather than ninja:

> Inside the camp at Magari of the *shōgun* Yoshihisa there were *shinobi* whose names were famous throughout the land. When Yoshihisa attacked Rokkaku Takayori, the family of Kawai Aki-no-kami of Iga, who served him at Magari earned considerable merit as *shinobi* in front of the great army of the *shōgun*. Since then successive generations of Iga men have been admired. This is the origin of the fame of the men of Iga.[3]

The reference to the names of Rokkaku Takayori and the *shōgun* Ashikaga Yoshihisa, who reigned from 1474 until 1489, enables us to identify this action as one fought in the year 1487, which was a decade after the end of one of the pivotal events in samurai history: the War of Ōnin.

The terrible Ōnin War, which lasted from 1467 until 1477, had begun over a succession dispute for the shogunate within the ruling Ashikaga family, in which the aforementioned Yoshihisa was, as an innocent baby, one of the rival claimants. It was a war which was fought with fire and starvation as much as with sword and bow, and it had devastated both the Capital and the prestige of the *bakufu*. The war had now been over for ten years, and Yoshihisa, who had been raised to the position of *shōgun* at the age of nine years by his father Yoshimasa, took steps to restore his family's military prowess as soon as he was of an age to do so.

His chance came in 1487 – or possibly in 1488 (chronicles are in conflict on the date).

The outlaw Ishikawa Goemon
Ishikawa Goemon is one of several bandits associated with the Iga/Ise area to whom has been credited expertise in ninjutsu. *Goemon was eventually arrested and boiled to death in a cauldron. (From* Ehon Taikō-ki, *a romance based on the life of Toyotomi Hideyoshi by Takenouchi Kakusai, and illustrated by Okada Gyokuzan; published in Osaka by Kobayashi Rokubei in Kyōwa 2 [1802]; private collection.)*

That year, some 46 of the landowners of Ōmi province, including a number from Koga, appealed to the *shōgun* against the excesses of the *shugo* of Ōmi, Rokkaku Takayori, who was in the process of seizing everyone else's lands for himself. This in itself was nothing remarkable. The *shugo* were the provincial governors appointed by the Ashikaga, and the disorder of the Ōnin War had enabled many a *shugo* to disregard his obligation to the *shōgun* and treat the territory entrusted to him as his own. These warlords now called themselves *daimyō* (great names) and such was the intensity of petty wars between *daimyō* that the period between about 1480 and 1600 has been dubbed the *sengoku-jidai*, the Age of the Country at War. But a proud young *shōgun*, the most warlike of his family for a century, did not see such presumption as inevitable, and would not tolerate it. He therefore took personal charge of an expedition against Rokkaku Takayori and besieged him in his castle at Kannon-ji in Ōmi province.

Young Yoshihisa made camp at the nearby village of Magari. He was joined by several allies sympathetic to the cause of the shogunate and made good progress, but unfortunately Yoshihisa's physical health was not the equal of his mental condition. He was taken ill at camp, and succumbed to a sickness from which he was eventually to die. His army, therefore, struck camp and returned to Kyōto. Following his untimely death he was succeeded as *shōgun* by his cousin Yoshitane who returned to the fray in 1491 and defeated Rokkaku.

Sugiyama comments that there is no conclusive proof for the use of ninja at the Magari camp, and presents as circumstantial evidence against it the observation that Rokkaku Takayori, when attacked by Yoshihisa and Yoshitane, repeatedly withdrew in the direction of Koga and Iga, and that the pursuing shogunal forces appear to have had little support from this direction. Alternatively, of course, this can be taken as evidence supporting the mercenary nature of the men of Iga and Koga who, as we shall see later, were willing to fight both for and against the same *daimyō* within a comparatively short space of time.

The campaign against the Rokkaku is mentioned in a recent interesting article which looks at the archaeological evidence presented by the numerous fortifications of Koga. Of the 21 hilltop castle sites identified, many date from early in the Sengoku Period, evidence of tremendous military activity at the time. The author also mentions the *kyōwasei* or 'republicanism' of Koga, whereby the various families were joined in a complex hierarchy of mutual support, thereby providing the ideal conditions for mercenary activity to flourish. The Wada family, for example, controlled a series of mountain-top fortresses along a river valley, and Wada Koremasa (1536–83) was sufficiently strong in Koga to give refuge there to the future *shōgun* Yoshiaki after the suicide of his brother Ashikaga Yoshiteru in 1565.[4]

A Monk Takes Note of Ninja

Moving on 60 years from the *Nochi Kagami* account, there is much better evidence for the use of ninja from Iga in a reliable chronicle which also presents them in a now familiar guise. The journal is the *Tamon-In nikki*, a diary kept by the Abbot Eishun of Tamon-In, a priory of the great Kōfuku-ji monastery of Nara. The monasteries took great pains to keep themselves informed of events in the provinces, and records such as the *Tamon-In nikki* are valuable source material. The entry for the twenty-sixth day of the eleventh month of the tenth Year of Tembun (1541) reads as follows:

The Iga *shū* entered Kasagi castle in secret and set fire to a few of the priests' quarters. They also set fire to outbuildings in various places inside the *San no maru*. They captured the *Ichi no maru* and the *Ni no maru*.

This castle was on the same Mount Kasagi that was defended during the Nambokuchō Wars, and which fell to a similar attack. *Maru* refers to the various defensive rings equivalent to the baileys of a European castle. *Shū* means 'unit' or 'band'.

The chronicle goes on to identify the defender of Kasagi castle as a certain Kizawa Nagamasa, which allows us to sketch in some more details about the circumstances surrounding the action. Kizawa Nagamasa was a *daimyō*, one of the petty princelings who had benefited from the breakdown of central control during the Ōnin War, and had some influence over Yamato and Kawachi provinces. In 1540, when the Age of the Country at War was at its height, his territory was invaded by the ambitious 17-year-old Miyoshi Chōkei, assisted by his great-uncle Masanaga and various allies. The Kizawa army took up a position on Kasagi, where they were attacked by Miyoshi's ally Tsutsui

The ninja!
The traditional image of the ninja is illustrated by this 'posed' scene photographed at Iga-Ueno castle. The actor is dressed in the well-known black costume with a headcowl. (Courtesy of the Iga-Ueno Department of Tourism.)

Junshō, so it is presumably Tsutsui Junshō who uses the Iga *shū* against the defenders. The men of Iga were worthy of their hire, for Kizawa Nagamasa was mortally wounded, and the castle soon fell.[6]

(It is interesting to note the presence inside Kasagi castle with Kizawa of a very famous family from the locality – the Yagyū. They were represented in the person of Yagyū Ieyoshi, father of Muneyoshi, who was later to found one of the most celebrated schools of swordsmanship in Japan. Yagyū village lay at the foot of Mount Kasagi, and when Kasagi fell the Yagyū continued the struggle, young Muneyoshi fighting the first battle of his life against the Tsutsui in 1544. A century later Muneyoshi's grandson Jūbei Mitsuyoshi was to have tales told about his exploits as a ninja, so it is fascinating to see the family on the receiving end of ninjutsu in 1541.)[7]

Ieyasu and the Ninja of Koga

We mentioned briefly at the start of this chapter the intimate relationship that grew between the future *shōgun* Tokugawa Ieyasu and the inhabitants of Iga and Koga, some of whom were to become hereditary palace guards to the Tokugawa family. The way in which this relationship developed over the years provides some of the best written evidence available for the activites of ninja during the sixteenth century. The bond between the Tokugawa and the Iga ninja is closely connected with the disastrous Iga Revolt of 1579–81, which will be covered in Chapter 6, but the employment of the Koga ninja is much more straightforward, and also very well recorded.

However, it is first necessary to say a few words about Tokugawa Ieyasu himself. He was of an ancient family, as befitted a man who was to rise to the highest political office in the land, but the adolescent years of the future *shōgun* gave little indication of the greatness that was eventually to be his. The Matsudaira (the name Ieyasu bore until 1567) were in fact only minor *daimyō* based in the province of Mikawa on the Tōkaidō, squeezed awkwardly between the powerful warlords of Oda and Imagawa, and Ieyasu spent much of his childhood as hostage of one side or the other. This practice, which he suffered along with many of his contemporaries, guaranteed to whoever held the hostages the continued loyal service of the ally, lest, at the first sign of bad faith, the victims' throats be cut. Ieyasu was such a guest of the Imagawa on achieving manhood, and his status changed from that of being a helpless pawn to that of fighting in the Imagawa army. He rose rapidly through the ranks, and in 1560 fought on the Imagawa's behalf one element of a campaign that was designed to allow Imagawa Yoshimoto to achieve the supreme prize: a march on Kyōto, and subsequent control of the shogunate. The route was the Tōkaidō, and the territory of their arch-enemy Oda Nobunaga was the first hostile ground the army had to cross.

The resulting action, the Battle of Okehazama, was one of the most decisive battles in Japanese history, and a textbook action based on the principles of Sun Tzu, involving deception, forced marching, and an entire dummy army. Although outnumbered by twelve to one the young Oda Nobunaga outflanked the Imagawa army and raided Yoshimoto's camp under cover of a fortuitous thunderstorm. Yoshimoto was decapitated in the rush, and resistance collapsed. It was fortunate for the future Tokugawa Ieyasu that he was not present at Yoshimoto's headquarters, having been ordered by him to rest his troops in a frontier fort they had just taken.[8]

With the death of his overlord, Ieyasu was theoretically free of the obligation to serve the Imagawa that had been his for practically the whole of his life. He was too weak to operate as a *daimyō* on his own, so there was now a strong temptation to ally himself immediately with the all-conquering Oda, but the late Imagawa Yoshimoto had a son, Ujizane, who, while not enjoying the military skills of his father, possessed something far more likely to ensure the Tokugawa's continuing service. This was the presence in his castle at Sumpu of a number of hostages from Ieyasu's own family, including his wife and son, whose throats would surely be cut at the least indication of a change of allegiance. Ieyasu acted cautiously, and made a secret alliance with Oda Nobunaga while keeping up the outward appearance of continued loyalty to the Imagawa. But the prudent Ieyasu was soon placed in a dilemma. Oda Nobunaga began to seek concrete proof that he was willing to serve him, and Ujizane demanded nothing less than the same loyalty

Tokugawa Ieyasu
The future shōgun Tokugawa Ieyasu (1542–1616) made very good use of a group of ninja from Koga in 1562, when they were instrumental in taking the castle of Kaminojō from the Udono family. The sons of the Udono were taken hostage, and exchanged for Ieyasu's own family who were held by the Imagawa. The breaking of his alliance with Imagawa left Ieyasu free to join Oda Nobunaga, and it is from this time that his fortunes begin to improve considerably. A letter from Ieyasu praising those who took part in the attack is an important document for ninja activity. This fine modern bronze statue of him is in the grounds of Okazaki Castle. (Author's collection.)

Ieyasu had once given to his father. Both problems were solved by one dramatic stroke in the year 1562, with a little help from ninja.

The Imagawa had as their western outpost a castle called Kaminojō, which was held for them by a certain Udono Nagamochi. It promised to be a useful prize for the Oda, and if Ieyasu was able to capture it quickly on Nobunaga's behalf it would serve one additional purpose, because any hostages taken from Kaminojō could be exchanged for Ieyasu's own family. It would of course have to be done quickly before the news got out and Imagawa had a chance to murder them, so Ieyasu appointed his retainer Matsui Sakon Tadatsugu as commander of a force to make a swift attack. The source for the action, the *Mikawa Go Fudo-ki*, takes the story on:

The *monogashira* Mitsuhara Sanza'emon said: 'As this castle is built upon a formidable precipice we will be condemning many of our allies to suffer great losses. But by good fortune there are among the *go-hatamoto* some men associated with the Koga *shū* of Ōmi Province. Summon the Koga *shū* through their compatriots and then they can sneak into the castle'.[9]

Note how the expertise of the Koga *shū* in attacking castles is recognised as being a speciality they can offer. The leader of the men of Koga was a certain Tomo Tarōza'emon Sukeie (Yamaguchi says Tomo Yoshichirō Sukesada), who engaged over 80 soldiers experienced in *shinobi* work. (Yamaguchi adds a further 200 supplied by Ukai Magoroku).[10]

This group were ordered to lie down and hide in several places, and on the night of the fifteenth day of the third month sneaked inside the castle. Before long they were setting fire to towers inside the fortress.[11]

In other words, they carried out a classic ninja raid under cover of darkness. The *Mikawa Go-Fudo-ki* account, however, adds some interesting points of detail. First, the raiding party deliberately did not speak, (Yamaguchi says 'did not give their battle-shout on entering') as they ran around killing, so that the defenders thought they were traitors from within the garrison. Yamaguchi adds a further fascinating note by stating that the ninja dressed like the defenders, the better to cause confusion, and as they spread out communicated with one another by using a password. (If it proves nothing else, at least it shows that on this occasion the ninja were not dressed in black!) Their leader was also apparently carrying a spear, which cannot have been very convenient for climbing rocks.[12]

. . . the garrison were utterly defeated and fled. The keeper of the castle, Nagamochi, fled to beside the Gomadō (the 'Hall of Prayers') on the north side of the castle, where Tomo Yoshichirō Sukesada discovered his whereabouts, came running up, thrust his spear at him, and took his head as he lay prostrate. His sons Fujitarō Nagateru and Katsusaburō Nagatada were captured alive by Tomo Hoki-no-kami Suketsuna.[13]

Two hundred of the Udono garrison were burned to death in the conflagration which followed.

Thus, Ieyasu had the castle and had demonstrated his loyalty to Nobunaga, but this was of less importance to him than the priceless reward of Udono's two sons as hostages. He proposed an exchange of prisoners to Imagawa Ujizane, who most unwisely accepted. Once reunited with his immediate family Ieyasu was free to make alliances with whomsoever he chose, and it is from this moment that his ascendancy begins.

Following his account of the battle, Yamaguchi quotes a *kanjō* (letter of commendation), sent by Ieyasu to Tomo Sukesada praising the service he has rendered at Kaminojō, and preserved in the archives of the Iwane, a prominent family of Koga:

This is concerning the time when Udono Fujitarō Nagateru was defeated. Such renown has not been equalled in recent times. Since that time I have been occupied with one thing and another and have neglected to write for some years. (I wish you) good health, and have the honour to congratulate you. I have been pleased to listen to the particulars of the matter despatched by both my retainers Matsui Sakon Tadatsugu and Sakai Masachika.[14]

Little is known about this document, and even the date is uncertain; but Yamaguchi states that it is genuine, and as the only *kanjō* in history addressed to a leader of ninja, provides unique written proof of the value Ieyasu placed on their particular abilities.

The affair of the two surviving sons of Udono was not however, quite over. As part of the hostage agreement Ieyasu allowed Imagawa Ujizane to keep what was left of Kaminojō castle, and after its repair Ujizane re-appointed the brothers to its defence. Having already suffered one defeat at the hands of Ieyasu the pair began a rather unwise policy of outwardly supporting the raids into Mikawa province by the Buddhist fanatics of the Ikkō sect. The raids went as far as Okazaki, Ieyasu's capital, which particularly infuriated a certain relation of Ieyasu whose relatives, including a daughter, had been held hostage

Planning a ninja raid
The incident depicted here cannot be identified, as the actual print is two pages of an illustrated book which has been taken apart in order to sell the pictures individually – an unfortunate practice by unscrupulous dealers, which has led to the loss of many fine works. The two men in conversation would appear to be ninja planning a raid across the moat, using the hooked rope which one of them is carrying. Their scheme has been overheard by a man called Gorosuke, but nothing further can be concluded. (Private collection.)

in Yoshida by the Imagawa. They had not been part of the deal struck over the fall of Kaminojō, and had subsequently been put to death by the unpleasant business of impaling on sharp stakes. This man, Matsudaira Kiyoyoshi, launched a furious attack on Kaminojō castle:

But, as might be expected, the Udono brothers defended it vigorously, and the attackers were thoroughly beaten, many being either wounded or killed in action. On hearing that the attacking force were on the point of being defeated His Lordship set out in great haste, set up his army in camp on Natoriyama, and sent men of Koga who attacked the castle. Taking advantage of an unguarded point they made a commotion in the castle as Ieyasu had ordered them to. The Udono brothers had run out of defensive techniques. Fujitarō gathered seven samurai about him, but when they were all killed the castle fell. Ieyasu ordered his men to return to Ōkazaki.[15]

That was the end of the Udono brothers, who thus earned their place in history by being probably the only samurai to have been defeated by the same ninja twice!

The Rokkaku Family and the Ninja of Iga

The picture that emerges from the above accounts is therefore one of a growing tradition in Iga and Koga of providing a particular form of service, consisting above all of a specialised knowledge of castle-entry techniques. During the 1560s, at least, there appear to be no rules governing in whose service the ninja would perform. It was simply a case of supply meeting demand, and the conditions of the Age of War ensured a steady demand.

It is not unreasonable to ask what the ninja themselves got out of it, for the men of Koga and Iga clearly owed no vassal allegiance to any of the *daimyō* they served. This service must therefore have been that of paid mercenaries, which is supported by the use of such words as 'hired', 'employed' and so on, although the nature of the payment that changed hands remains a mystery. The whole topic of money was however regarded by samurai in general as unspeakably vulgar, so this is perhaps not so surprising. Nevertheless, the curious example which follows of the Rokkaku family of Ōmi province provides the strongest evidence so far that the ninja of Iga and Koga are the sole examples of mercenaries in the history of the samurai.

An earlier member of the Rokkaku family, Rokkaku Takayori, was mentioned at the beginning of this chapter for having had *shinobi* used against him by the *shōgun* Yoshihisa in 1487. His grandson Rokkaku Yoshikata was the family head until his retirement in 1562, and sometime between 1558 (the year he adopted the name Yoshikata) and 1562 he fought a campaign against the treacherous retainer whose name (amusing to English ears), was Dodo. The story is told in the *Bansen Shūkai*.[16] Dodo had rebelled against his *daimyō* and entrenched himself within Sawayama castle, the site of which is near the present town of Hikone. In spite of a siege that lasted many days Yoshikata could not budge him, and decided to employ a ninja from Iga called Tateoka no Dōshun. Dōshun, like many ninja, was a believer in the magic arts, and on the way from Iga called in to have his fortune told by a diviner called Miyasugi. Miyasugi worked out that Dōshun was destined for good luck, and presented him with a poem in his honour:

Sawayama ni Dodo to naru ikazuchi mo,
Igasaki ireba ochi ni keru kana.

By means of several puns the poem refers to the fall of Sawayama castle and Dodo with it. Thunder is also involved. Dōshun was most impressed and changed his name accordingly to Igasaki Dōshun, from the second line of the poem. Thus spiritually uplifted he led into action his team of 48 ninja, of whom 44 were from Iga and four from Koga. Dōshun proposed using a ninja technique called *bakemono-jutsu*, (ghost technique), which provided a simple way of walking into Dodo's castle unseen. What Dōshun did was to steal one of the *chōchin* (paper lanterns) that bore Dodo's family *mon* or badge. His ninja constructed several replicas, and Dōshun and his men calmly walked straight in at the front gate. They then started to set fire to the castle. Dodo's garrison concluded that traitors had emerged from their own midst, and in spite of heroic efforts to extinguish the fire panic began to spead as quickly as the flames. At this point Rokkaku Yoshikata ordered his main army into a victorious final assault.

Nothing better illustrates the mercenary nature of the ninja than the fact that in 1561 (which is certainly within two years of the above incident) we see the Asai family using a

Rokkaku Yoshikata
Rokkaku (or Sasaki) Yoshikata used ninja from Iga against his enemy Dodo sometime around the year 1560. Within two years, Yoshikata was to have ninja from the same province used against him, which strongly supports the notion of the ninja of Iga as being paid mercenaries. Yoshikata, incidentally, was the founder of a renowned school of the martial arts known as the Sasaki-ryū. (From Toyotomi eimei hyaku yūden; *by a pupil of Kuniyoshi; private collection.)*

different unit of Iga ninja against the same Rokkaku Yoshikata! Asai Nagamasa (1545–73) was another of the classic *sengoku-daimyō*. He must have been very familiar with the local ninja clans, because his territory was northern Ōmi province, and he was the grandson of an earlier Asai who had carved the territory out in the face of strong opposition from Yoshikata's grandfather Rokkaku Takayori. The Asai's war with the Rokkaku thus went on for three generations, and in 1561 Asai Nagamasa resolved to re-take the castle of Futō (now Maibara) to the east of Lake Biwa, which had recently fallen to the Rokkaku.

The castle had been placed in the care of two generals, neither of whom appears to have been very competent. Nagamasa ordered an attack, and placed matters in the capable hands of two commanders called Imai Kenroku and Isono Tamba-no-kami. They in turn engaged the assistance of three men from Iga called Shima Wakasa-no-kami, Iwakō Chikuzen-no-kami and Kanda Shurito to provide a night attack which would complement the more conventional assault planned by the others. It is interesting to note the high rank implied by the suffix *no-kami*, the sinecurial title meaning 'Lord of'. Yamaguchi (who gets the date wrong) quotes two chronicles which summarise the initial events. In his quote from the *Shima Kiroku* we read: 'The Iga *shū* entered in secret, started fires in the castle, and at this signal the keep and second bailey were conquered.'[17] And in the quote from the *Asai Sandai-ki*: 'We employed *shinobi-no-mono* of Iga . . . They were contracted to set fire to the castle.'[18]

Such are the bare bones of the action, but things did not go quite according to plan. Using the *Asai Sandai-ki*, with additional material from the *Shima Kiroku*, Yamaguchi has reconstructed the confusing events of the night of the first day of the seventh month. The Iga *shinobi* were in position, and the 'conventional forces' had begun to move forward. But it soon became clear to Imai Kenroku, who was stationed on a nearby hill, that the *shinobi* had not moved to order. When he complained about their hesitation he received the reply that a samurai from north of Lake Biwa could not possibly understand *shinobi* tactics, and that he would have to wait for a propitious moment. But by now the

Asai Nagamasa
Asai Nagamasa (1541–73) hired ninja from Iga to help him retake the castle of Futō (now Maibara) which had fallen to Rokkaku Yoshikata. The campaign nearly ended in disaster when one of his commanders, a certain Imai Kenroku, impatient that the ninja were taking so long to raid the castle, attempted a night manoeuvre which brought him across the front of an allied contingent. A fight broke out between them, during which Kenroku was killed. (From a nineteenth-century copy of the original painting; courtesy of the Jōzai-ji, Gifu.)

army was on the move. The fire attack was late, and the *shinobi*, in the manner of mercenaries the world over, implied by their refusal to attack until ready that unless allowed to conduct warfare in their own way they would all go home. The *shinobi* leader Shima Wakasa-no-kami suggested that Imai Kenroku regroup his forces. If he withdrew for about an hour, the *shinobi* would raid the castle, and the signal to move forward would be fire appearing from it.

This Imai Kenroku agreed to do, but the results were almost disastrous. His army blundered across the front of his comrade Isono Tamba-no-kami, who appears not to have been informed about the manoeuvre. The samurai of the latter army drew the conclusion that a dawn attack had been made on them from the castle. A quick-thinking horseman in the front line called Kishizawa Yoichi sprang into action in an attempt to achieve the 'Holy Grail' of samurai warfare by being first into the battle. In addition to such chance of glory he observed, riding just ahead of him, the 'enemy' commander. He galloped forward and the unfortunate Imai Kenroku, trying desperately to control the night march of his army, received Yoichi's spear thrust in his back. Being totally un- prepared for any assault, as he knew there were only friendly troops behind him, he was too shocked to give any resistance, and quickly fell dead from his horse. The two armies began fighting each other, and 20 were killed before order was restored. By then the ninja had set fire to the castle, and the two shattered allies joined forces to attack it. Futō eventually fell, to everyone's relief, but at the price of this wasteful loss of one of the Asai's best commanders.

We may conclude, therefore, that the traditional pre-eminence claimed by Iga and Koga for selling their ninja activities has a sound basis in fact. But this is not the whole of the story, for equally successful examples of ninja operations were being carried out elsewhere in Japan without a mercenary connection, and this will be the subject of the chapter which follows.

4 THE LOYAL NINJA

There are several excellent accounts of ninja use in sixteenth-century Japan that appear to have no connection with either Iga or Koga. The background, however, is the same: the breakdown of Shogunal authority after the Ōnin War, and the growth of a *daimyō*'s territories at the expense of rivals. The difference is that the use of ninja who are not from Iga or Koga appears to have no mercenary aspect. Instead the ninja bands are retained followers of a *daimyō* who receive a stipend. In each of the four accounts which follow, the *shinobi* are an integral part of the *daimyō*'s army, and are used as spies, or as small groups of obviously élite forces whose purpose is to cause havoc and confusion in the enemy ranks, either when the enemy is in prepared siege lines or conducting field operations.

The earliest account is of the 1540s, which makes it contemporary with the *Tamon-In nikki* record quoted earlier. Sasama, in fact, quotes it as an example of the use of Iga ninja, but this does not appear to be justified from a reading of the original.[1] It occurs in a chronicle called the *Chūgoku Chiran-ki*, which is a record of the wars fought between the families of Mōri and Amako on the shores of the Inland Sea. The pattern is a familiar one, as the Mōri extend their territory at the expense of lesser fry like the young *daimyō* Amako Haruhisa (1514–62). Haruhisa appears to have been most unwisely belligerent, and the result of his aggression against the Mōri led to many of his retainers abandoning him for service to the Ōuchi. A generation of warfare ensued, from which the Mōri emerged eventually victorious and the Amako were obliterated. The use by the Mōri of *shinobi* occurs early on in the chronicle, during one of Haruhisa's aggressive spells:

. . . on the 4th day of the 9th month of Tembun 9 (1540) Haruhisa set off to Yoshida no Koriyama with over 70,000 men. Koriyama being a large mountain, there were seven ways up it. He came forward to Yoshida Kamimura, and burned it so that not even one house remained. On the 6th day of the same, he burned to the ground Tarōmaru no machi, and the *ashigaru* spent the day fighting.

On the 12th day of the same, after they had burned the byways, the leader of the Mōri side *ashigaru* called Watanabe Tarōza'emon, struggled with the Amako side's *ashigaru* general at the main castle. At the main castle he was struck and died. *Ashigaru* of the Mōri side, Ihara, Hizume (Gyōbu Shōyū) and Watanabe Genjūrō were killed in action.

On the 23rd day of the same, the Amako took up position on Aoyama and Mitsutsukayama. *Shinobi* soldiers were sent out from the Mōri side, and they split the Kazakoshiyama force.[2]

That brief reference is the only clue we have to the use Mōri made of their *shinobi*. On the face of it they would appear to have been a sort of commando unit from within the Mōri army, rather than hired mercenaries.

The *kusa* in action
Kusa *(grass) is the alternative word to* shinobi *which is used in the* Hōjō Godai-ki *to describe the hidden sentries employed by the Satake against the Hōjō in 1575. The* kusa *lay down in the grass to intercept the enemy's mounted scouts when they came on reconnaissance. Note how the* kusa *are not dressed in black, and spring up 'like a swarm of bees' as the scouts approach. (From a woodblock-printed edition of the* Hōjō Godai-ki; Manji 2 [1659], *private collection.)*

Ninja in the Kantō

To judge from the available evidence the activities of the mercenary Iga/Koga ninja do not seem to have included intelligence gathering, which is in line with the recommendation of Sun Tzu that the successful agent should be very close to the general who uses him. The great *daimyō* Takeda Shingen, for example, made extensive use of spies for obtaining intelligence about his rival Uesugi Kenshin, and none appears to have been employed as a mercenary from outside. Instead they were all retainers of his loyal generals, but it is interesting to note that the Takeda took the extra precaution of taking hostage the spies' wives and children. Shingen had evidently read his Sun Tzu and the warning about double agents! He had three units of secret agents, consisting of ten men each under the three generals Amari, Itagaki and Iidomo. Information brought to the attention of the three generals was despatched by fast-riding horsemen to Shingen's headquarters in Kofu.[3]

An expert horseman could provide an excellent intelligence service on his own, particularly when two armies were taking up battle positions, and the exploits of 'warrior-

The scouts' escape
This illustration concludes the story of the warrior-scouts and the kusa. *Yamakami San'emonnojō escapes from the* kusa *by spurring his horse up the slopes of a mountain. His comrade Haga Hikojirō swims his horse across the river. (From a woodblock-printed edition of the* Hōjō Godai-ki; Manji 2 [1659]; *private collection.)*

scouts' form the first of two dramatic accounts in the *Hōjō Godai-ki*, the chronicle of the exploits of the five generations of the Hōjō family, compiled sometime about 1600 by a former Hōjō retainer, Miura Jōshin. The history of the Hōjō encompasses most of the features that made the *daimyō* the warlords that they were. The first to bear the name, Hōjō Sōun, rose from a position of service under another *daimyō* to a position where he could pass on to his son and heir two complete provinces. The territory increased under the subsequent two *daimyō*, until by the late 1580s the family controlled much of the Kantō plain, the fertile flatlands across much of which modern Tōkyō now sprawls.

The first account refers to the use in 1575 of ninja, here called *shinobi*, and also *kusa*, or grass, against the Hōjō by the Satake, a rival whom the Hōjō confronted on several occasions. Apart from acting as spies, the Satake's *kusa* had a very specific extra role. Acting in effect as hidden sentries, they would conceal themselves around the edges of an army camp and try to intercept the enemy's mounted scouts who were carrying out their own rapid intelligence gathering operation. One might perhaps regard them as anti-ninja ninja!

. . . after we had set up camp, men went out as scouts to familiarise themselves with the locality. These were highly trained horsemen, and were exclusively persons of great merit. The warrior scouts would ride to the boundaries, looking for any signs, or would head up a slope on to high ground from which they could survey the enemy flags, and then hurriedly return to our lines.

However (it was also the practice that) when a general had set off to war, and spread out his army against the opposing forces, he would send out *ashigaru* to the enemy front line opposite to the camp, where they lay down in the grass and spied on the enemy, then returned at dawn. They were called *kusa* or *shinobi*. Some of these night-time *kusa* would remain until noon of the following day. Our warrior scouts were unaware of this, and when they went past the 'forward line' the *kusa* would spring up, cutting off their means of retreat, and try to seize them and kill them. On such occasions, as they were skilled horsemen, they would ride hard away, heedless of plain or mountain.

Jōshin then describes this particular use of *kusa* in 1575:

We had taken up a position far away from the enemy, where there was water, in a low-lying depression at the foot of Mount Taisan. It was at the edge of a large river and in the shade of a forest. Behind these features the lines were arranged in the *gyōrin-kakuyoku* formation.[4] In spite of being under the command of the *musha-bugyō* the scouts were left to their own devices, and one night even rode to the earthwork palisades of the camp. It was an act of daring.

It was the autumn of 1575 and Satake Yoshinobu and Hōjō Ujinao were confronting each other in Shimotsuke Province, and flags fluttered to east and to west. Ujinao selected five horsemen from among his *hatamoto* and made them scouts. They rode off towards the border where the enemy flags were flying. Among them were two horsemen, Yamakami San'emonnojō and Haga Hikojirō, who were familiar with the area. They rode hard to one *chō* from the boundary and rode up to a high place. Then they saw the enemy's *kusa*. They rose up like bees to surround the two mounted men and catch them like fish in a net. They made to take the horse of San'emonnojō, but in spite of being in enemy territory he turned his horse to the north and whipped it up to make a remarkable escape from the place, and rode hard for the flat plains, being chased across the grass, and while in flight he took one head. With many enemy in pursuit, being a strong horseman he rode up a large mountain, descended from its top, and rode on into friendly territory.

Hikojirō was surrounded by many enemies, and it was almost certain he would fall, having ridden into the area of the enemy camp, but he took the road through the ramparts and from here rode to the south. As he spurred on his mount horsemen set out from within the enemy camp from front and rear and from left and right, to capture him or cut him down. It was likely that he would be killed, but he struck his whip on the stirrups two or three times, and although his voice could be heard, several times he almost disappeared from sight. Finally he rode into the large river and made his horse swim, and arrived at the far bank.[5]

The account concludes with Hōjō Ujinao praising the two men, re-telling their exploits, and suitably rewarding them. There is a nice touch in that Miura Jōshin also refers to the bravery of the samurai's horses as being in no wit inferior to that of their riders.

The Battle Disrupters

The other account in the *Hōjō Godai-ki* refers to an action fought five years later by the above-mentioned fifth *daimyō* Ujinao, and on this occasion the use of ninja is carried out by the Hōjō themselves. The enemy are the Takeda family, and instead of *kusa* the ninja are called *rappa*, but it is clear from the context that their role is a classic ninja one of causing confusion to an enemy. The *rappa* leader was Kazama Kotarō, whose name can also be read as Fuma Kotarō, in which guise he appears in many popular works as one of the great ninja leaders of all time.

In olden times, as we have seen, when there was disorder in the Kantō, we always had bows and arrows at the ready. Now there were in those days rogues called *rappa*. These individuals were like thieves, but were not just thieves. These wicked people had brave and intelligent minds. . . . These people were granted a stipend in the provincial *daimyō*'s forces. Whatever the reasons for what they were called, all these *rappa* skilfully

44

investigated thieves in their own provinces, hunted them down and cut off their heads. They stole into neighbouring provinces. Mountain banditry, piracy, night attacks, robbery, and thieving were their skills. They were intelligent, and devised plots and plans unattainable by ordinary people. In the old accounts, they learnt awe-inspiring lies and were intelligent, combining the aspects of sage and thief.[6]

There follows an anecdote about two Chinese thieves, and then Jōshin sets the scene for us:

Hōjō Ujinao ruled the eight provinces of the Kantō, and all the neighbouring provinces were enemies, causing never-ending war. In the autumn of 1580 the father and son team of Takeda Katsuyori and Takeda Nobukatsu commanded the armies of Shinano, Kai and Suruga. They first moved into Sanmaibashi in Suruga, covering their flanks with the steep and dangerous Kisegawa. All the army set up camp on the plain of Ukishimagahara. Ujinao accordingly led his army of the eight provinces of the Kantō and made camp at Hatsune ga Hara and Mishima, in Izu. Ujinao had among his command two hundred *rappa* who received stipends, one of whom was an *akumono* ('wicked person'). His name was Kazama. He was regarded as the top villain with such extreme ways. Under Kazama were four leaders. . . . Two were mountain bandits or pirates, and two were robbers. The bandits were expert in mountains and rivers, the thieves broke into and entered enemy positions. The robbers (*settō*), were called *hosoru nusubito* (thin thieves) and had *shinobi* skills. These four leaders primarily made night attacks. Their unit of 200 men was divided into four sections, and went out whatever the weather, on wet nights or dry nights, still nights or windy nights.

Every night or so they crossed the great Kisegawa and entered secretly into Katsuyori's camp. They captured people alive, and cut through the ropes tethering the horses, which they rode bareback, plundering and raiding to ridiculous lengths. In their night attacks, moreover, they set fire to things, and raised the allies' battlecry to make them think they were friends. All the camp was in uproar and shock. Armour belonging to one was fought over by two or three others with fierce arguments. Panicking to get out they were led astray to front and rear. Thinking them enemies they turned against friends, killing each other, scattering fires, and putting all their plans into disorder, completely confused. When dawn broke they examined the heads of the slain, and discovered that in the fighting low ranking soldiers had taken the heads of their lords, and children had taken the heads of fathers.[7]

The disgrace felt by the Takeda was considerable. However, a small group was determined to take revenge, even on such elusive opponents:

Having lost all honour they cut off their pigtails and renounced the world, meaning to ascend the peak of Mount Koya. But ten men had been outside and although urged to cut off their pigtails said: 'There is no justification in continuing to live at all. We will cut open our bellies.' But one man stepped forward and said: 'By our death we would be apologising for the sins of destroying our lords and killing our parents, and surely we are being punished for committing the five evil things and the eight cruel things. But this would be to avoid our duty and take the easy way. We must fight the two hundred men who attacked us.'

'Kazama Kotarō is the general of the *rappa*. We should lay down our lives by killing him. This evening he will come for another night attack. We will wait by the road by which they will come. They will be dispersed, so we will mingle with them in the confusion until they come together. Kazama is a giant who cannot be concealed among his two hundred men. He is 7 *shaku* 2 *sun* in height, with roughly hewn sinews in his arms and legs. His intelligence raises him above the common herd. His eyes appear to be upside down, he has black whiskers, and his mouth is particularly wide at the sides. Four of his "fangs" stick out. His head resembles Fukurokuju, his nose is uplifted, and if he raises his voice it can be heard 50 *chō* away, but if he speaks quietly it is a tiny whisper. This is how you will recognise him easily. When you discover Kazama, grab him forcefully, thus realising your ambition in the world of taking revenge on the account to our deceased lords and dead parents, so that hell will have no charge to lay before them.'

So, by the road along which they would travel, the ten men waited in the grass. Kazama carried out his night attack, and the ten men mingled with them. But, fatefully, when those taking part in the attack gathered together, they lit pine torches, and at a prearranged signal, suddenly stood up. Those who had mingled with them in accordance with their plan were unaware of this, and at another word they sat down, so the ten were caught and killed.[8]

This clever arrangement meant the end of any planned resistance to the *rappa*, who proceeded to keep the Takeda in a state of nervous tension for a long time to come. Rumours began to fly about. Note in particular the reference to Sun Tzu's *Art of War*:

Because this was happening night after night Katsuyori's men got very tired. As the nights ended they removed their armour and had a nap on the spot where they found themselves. One learned person said: 'When defending an area of flatland, if you see a flight of geese disturbed, according to ancient military writings it indicates soldiers hiding in the shelter of mountain slopes. Kazama is a *shinobi*. The *rappa* are probably still hiding in the grass.' The camp remained in a state of panic. When it got dark they attached the saddles to their horses and took their bows and arrows. They put the fuses into their arquebuses and kept their weapons under their pillows, wearing armour. This went on until the long nights of the third month of autumn, always repeating: 'That hateful Kazama is a *shinobi*. He may make a night attack!'[9]

Ninja in the North

So far we have seen examples of ninja use as far apart as the coast of the Inland Sea in the west of Japan and the area of Tōkyō in the east. The wars between the *daimyō* for control of Dewa and Mutsu, the most northerly provinces on the Japanese mainland, provide another example of how common was the use of *shinobi* skills. It is a remarkable account of a ninja being used by a castle garrison against its besiegers, a neat reversal of the usual situation. It is also a subtle exercise in psychological warfare!

The chronicle is the *Ōu Eikyo Gunki*, and the action described the heroic defence of the castle of Hataya by Eguchi Goenojō, loyal vassal of Mogami Yoshiakira (1546–1614):

. . . one of Yoshiakira's retainers called Eguchi Goenojō kept the castle of Hataya, on the Yonezawa road. When he heard of the treacherous gathering at Aizu, he immediately replastered the wall and deepened the ditch, piled up palisades, arrows and rice, and waited for the attack. . . . The vanguard were under the command of Kurogane Sonza'emonnojō, with 200–300 horsemen. He sounded the conch and the bell to signal the assault. As those in Hataya were approached by the enemy they attacked them vigorously with bows and guns. Seventy of the enemy were killed in one go, and many were wounded. The deaths led to a change of plan, and the army who had tried to take the castle came to a halt. Now there was within Hataya Castle a person with renowned *shinobi* skills, and that night he entered secretly into the enemy camp, and took the *sashimono* from Naoe Kanetsugu's guard within Kurogane Sonza'emonnojō's camp at Suikan, and planted it on a high point above the front gate of the castle. When dawn broke men from the attacking force saw it and said: 'This is mortifying. Not only has this tiny castle not fallen, but we have been so negligent that a flag has been stolen!'[10]

A *sashimono* was the personal flag worn for identification by a samurai on the back of his suit of armour. As the stolen one belonged to a guard it probably had emblazoned on it the personal *mon*, or badge, of the commander Naoe Kanetsugu (1570-1619), making its display as a trophy doubly mortifying. Such psychological ploys could have an effect on an army's morale, but this would be as nothing compared to the devastating consequences arising from the assassination by a ninja of a *daimyō*.

The Takeda samurai prepare to attack Fuma Kotarō
Fuma (or Kazama) Kotarō is one of the most celebrated of the historical ninja. He served the Hōjō, and the Hōjō Godai-ki records his activities as a battle disrupter against the Takeda in 1580. Night after night, Kotarō and his men would raid the Takeda camp, cause confusion and panic, and carry off loot. Eventually, a group of Takeda samurai decided to ambush Kotarō during one of his raids, and lay in wait. As the rappa *(the name used here for the ninja) approached, the Takeda men mingled with them; suddenly, at a pre-arranged signal, the* rappa *crouched down, thus disclosing the strangers among them. This picture, which is probably the earliest woodblock-printed illustration of a ninja, reflects the demonic description of the 'superman' Kotarō which is given in the text. (From a woodblock-printed edition of the* Hōjō Godai-ki; *Mani 2 [1659]; private collection.)*

47

The assassin
The context makes it unlikely that the assailant is anything other than an opportunist, but his use of a jūjutsu *armlock on his victim reminds one of the tremendous reputation ninja acquired for secret assassinations. (From* Ehon Taikō-ki, *a romance based on the life of Toyotomi Hideyoshi by Takenouchi Kakusai, and illustrated by Okada Gyokuzan; published in Ōsaka by Kobayashi Rokubei in Kyōwa 2 [1802]; private collection.)*

Assassination at Court
The Heike Monogatari *begins with the account of a thwarted assassination attempt that has all the hallmarks of a technique of* ninjutsu. *Being warned that his enemies intended his death, Tadamori produced a dagger as a warning that their plot was known to him, and calmly drew the blade through his hair. It was a grave offence to draw a weapon within the precincts of the Court, even for so admirable a purpose as saving one's own life; but when challenged Tadamori was able to show that the supposed dagger had only a wooden blade covered in silver, and his cleverness was much admired. (From the first volume of an early woodblock-printed edition of* Heike Monogatari, *in 12 volumes, illustrated by an unknown artist; Meireki 2 [1656]; private collection.)*

5 ASSASSINS

The previous chapters have dealt with two of the major rôles which ninja were called upon to perform during the turbulent years of Japan's 'Age of War', the carrying out of surprise attacks on castles, and the disruption and confusion of the enemy troops in field battles. But the best known of all ninja activities, and the one most exaggerated by fiction and romance, was the ninja's rôle as the silent and deadly assassin. This is the image of the ninja *par excellence*, dressed in black, sneaking into the castle at dead of night, and then polishing off his sleeping victim with knife or poison.

We have noted several examples of assassination so far, such as the killing of the *kumaso* chieftain by Prince Yamato, and it is curious to note that the *Heike Monogatari*, for all its concentration on the noble deeds of samurai in combat, begins with the thwarting of an assassination attempt by the sort of trick later to be attributed to skilled ninja. The intended victim was Taira Tadamori (1096–1153). He was the first of the Taira family to come to prominence at the Imperial court, and had risen rapidly in the favour of the Emperor. As a result he suffered from the jealousy of the other courtiers, who plotted to assassinate him during a forthcoming festival. Tadamori got to hear of what was afoot, and prepared accordingly:

Before entering the Court he provided himself with a long dagger which he girt on under his long court dress, and turning aside to a dimly lit place, slowly drew the blade and passed it through the hair of his head so that it gleamed afar off with an icy sheen, causing all to stare open-eyed.[1]

He also arranged for an armed retainer to be stationed outside, and the combination ensured that no attempt was made on his life. Yet the dramatic gestures he had made to ensure his safety seemed equally likely to procure his disgrace, because the wearing of weapons and the personal attendance of a guard were things that were against all precedent. The rival court nobles together petitioned that his name should be erased from the list of courtiers and that he be deprived of rank and office. Summoned to explain himself, Tadamori showed that the supposed dagger was actually a dummy made of wood, and this had been sufficient to save him. He was pardoned for the assumed offence, and it is interesting to note his companions praising Tadamori's deception.[2]

The First Ninja Assassination

Tadamori, of course, was no ninja, nor were any of the jealous rivals who had planned his downfall, and we have to turn to the later *gunkimono* the *Taiheiki* to find the dramatic incident that both Sasama[3] and Yamaguchi[4] regard as the earliest *shinobi* assassination in Japanese history.

The assassination is described in the section of the *Taiheiki* entitled, 'The Opinion of Nagasaki Shinsaemon-no-jō and the Matter of Master Kumawaka'. Master Kumawaka is the assassin in question, and was certainly not a professional ninja, but rather the 13-year-old son of a certain Lord Suketomo, who had been sent into exile on the island of Sado for his part in the conspiracy of Go-Daigo to overthrow the shogunate. The members of the *bakufu*, having decided to banish the sovereign likewise, determined to go further with the Emperor's fellow conspirators, and ordered that each be put to death. Hearing of this Kumawaka took leave of his mother, and with one servant as companion, made the long and difficult journey to Sado to be with his father before his execution.

Suketomo had been placed in the custody of the Lay Monk Homma Saburō, who had him confined to a house that was surrounded by a dense thicket of bamboo and protected by a moat and a wall. Although Kumawaka was not harmed when he arrived, Homma Saburō did not allow father and son actually to meet, and the first Kumawaka was to see of his father were his cremated remains following his execution on a distant dry riverbed. Kumawaka thus swore revenge on Homma Saburō, and determined to kill either Saburō or his son.

For someone who was not a professional assassin Kumawaka's preparations were commendably thorough. He first feigned illness so as not to be sent back to Kyōto with his father's mortal remains, and the apparent affliction also ensured for him a place within Homma Saburō's house. Thus began a brief period of intelligence gathering:

For four or five days Kumawaka lay in bed, as one afflicted in all his members. Yet secretly at night he stole forth to learn the place where Homma slept, thinking, 'If there is a chance, I will stab Homma or his son and rip open my belly.'[5]

He chose his moment well. It was a night of violent rain and wind, and the guards on duty were sleeping in their quarters beyond the courtyard. Homma Saburō had actually changed his sleeping room, but Kumawaka found it out, and was about to rush upon him when he remembered that he had not actually got a sword of his own, a strange omission for an assassin. Realising that he would have to do the deed with Saburō's own sword he was concerned that the light burning in the room would awaken him when Kumawaka attempted to draw it from its scabbard. The device he used to prevent this would have done credit to any ninja!

. . . gazing towards the lamp he beheld a multitude of moths clinging to the clear sliding doors (the season being summer). Thereupon, he set a door ajar, so that the insects entered in swarms, quickly putting out the light.[6]

Going up to Saburō, Kumawaka took the sleeping man's dagger, which he placed in his belt, and then slowly drew Saburō's sword. He held the point of the blade to his victim's chest, and kicked the pillow away:

When Homma awoke, Kumawaka drove in the sword steadily above his navel, all the way to the floor mat, and thrust it again into his throat. Then, showing no fear at all, he hid himself in a bamboo thicket to the rear.[7]

The words which the anonymous chronicler places in the mouths of the guards who come rushing to Saburō's aid depend upon which version of the text is used. McCullough's translation notes that 'they beheld small bloody footprints', which led them to conclude that a youth, undoubtedly Kumawaka, had done the deed. Sasama and Yamaguchi,

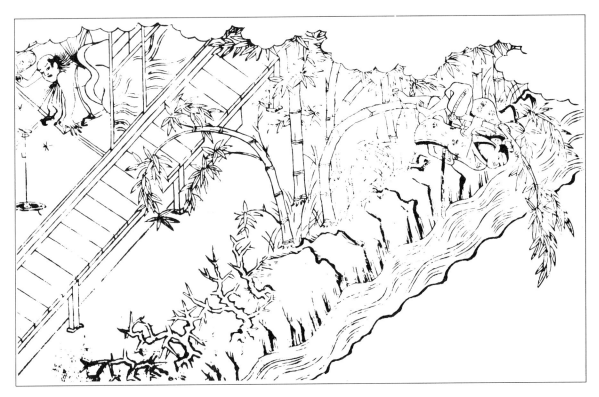

The death of Homma Saburō

One of the earliest written accounts of an assassination by night occurs in the Taiheiki, *when a youth called Kumawaka took revenge upon Homma Saburō, who had been responsible for the judicial murder of Kumawaka's father. The action has many* ninjutsu-*like features, such as the stratagem whereby Kumawaka douses the light in the room by letting in a swarm of insects. In this illustration, Kumawaka escapes by climbing up a tall bamboo, which bends under his weight and allows him to drop outside the compound. (From an early woodblock-printed edition of the* Taiheiki, *with illustrations by an unknown artist; Genroku 11 [1698]; private collection.)*

emphasising the ninja element, use a two-character compound meaning small-person, which we are instructed to read phonetically as *shinobi*. Kumawaka's escape from the bamboo thicket at the rear, in true ninja style, is illustrated in a seventeenth-century book illustration to the *Taiheiki*:

He thought to jump across the moat, yet in no wise might he do it, for it was six yards wide and more than ten feet deep. But then he climbed nimbly to the top of a black bamboo growing above the water, saying, 'I will cross by making a bridge of this'. And the tip thereof bent down to the other side, so that he crossed over easily.[8]

The insistence by Sasama and Yamaguchi that this is the first ninja assassination does not therefore seem to be borne out by a reading of the full text. But by the Sengoku Period such activities had become commonplace, or were at least perceived to be commonplace, and it is this sheer uncertainty that led to the fear of *shinobi* assassination being unquestionably a real one.

The Knife in the Dark
There are few *sengoku-daimyō* who were not subject to some form of assassination

attempt during their lifetimes. Takeda Shingen, Uesugi Kenshin, Oda Nobunaga and Toyotomi Hideyoshi all experienced attempts on their lives and survived, and powerful *daimyō* such as they were surrounded by loyal bodyguards who kept their lord under constant protection, never separated from him by more than a thin wood and paper screen. One may perhaps argue that assassination by silent, expert, professional killers was therefore the only chance that rivals had of extinguishing the rulers of the great monoliths which the *daimyō* territories had become by the 1570s. For example, the Takeda bodyguard numbered 6373, and, although the word used for them may more properly be taken to mean 'household troops', the safety of their lord's person was their first consideration. Some *daimyō* took their own precautions. Matsuura, the *daimyō* of Hirado island, kept a heavy club in his bathroom. Takeda Shingen, who apparently had two doors on his lavatory, is recorded as recommending that even when alone with his wife a *daimyō* should keep his dagger close at hand. Mōri Motonari reckoned that a *daimyō* should trust no-one, particularly relatives, a wise precept illustrated by the case of Saitō Toshimasa (1494–1556), who had made an early career change from Buddhist priest to oil merchant and became a *daimyō* in his own right by murdering his adoptive father. Hōjō Sōun acquired his base of Odawara castle by arranging for the young owner to be murdered while out hunting, and even the powerful Oda Nobunaga was eventually to meet his end from a night attack on his sleeping quarters by a rival, though it took a small army, rather than one ninja, to do it.

But the greatest fear was always reserved for the night-time visit from a single invisible and deadly assassin, and the measures taken against such an event can be seen in various locations in Japan to this day. A *daimyō* would be at his most vulnerable when recovering from wounds, for which purpose a number of 'secret springs' would be maintained. The Japanese have appreciated from very early days the healing power of natural springs, and the recuperation associated with them. Japan is dotted with hot spring resorts, and a *daimyō* would have his own, in distant locations deep in the mountains which ninja could not find. Takeda Shingen had three such springs where he retired to recover. Castles, of course, were very well defended. The well-preserved private quarters at Inuyama castle, for example, have wooden sliding doors at the rear behind which armed guards would be always at the ready,[9] and in fact an entire building could be 'ninja-proofed', as shown by the famous and extraordinary 'nightingale floor' built in to the design of Nijō castle in Kyōto when it was erected for Tokugawa Ieyasu in 1600. As thousands of tourists discover every year, it is impossible to walk along the highly polished corridors without raising the tuneful squeaking from the carefully counter-balanced floorboards that was likened to the sound of a nightingale singing, and gave its own warning of an approaching assassin. The Tokugawa family were also helped by the clothes which were required to be worn at the *shōgun*'s court. The long *naga-bakama*, the wide trousers that actually covered the feet and had to be dragged behind as one walked, made an assassination attempt on the *shōgun* almost a physical impossibility.

The accounts which follow of ninja assassination attempts on *daimyō* have in common the interesting feature that the assassin has been sent by another *daimyō*! The well-defended Takeda Shingen had an attempt made on his life by a ninja called Hachisuka Tenzō sent by Oda Nobunaga. Having failed in his attempt Tenzō was forced to flee, and the Takeda samurai pursued him into a wood, where he concealed himself from the

A ninja creeps along the corridor
This is another splendid publicity photograph from Iga-Ueno, home of the historical ninja. The full details of the ninja's costume can be seen clearly. Note the sword over his shoulder, and the simple straw sandals. (Courtesy of the Iga-Ueno Department of Tourism.)

moonlight among the shadows of the trees. A spear thrust from his pursuers caught only his costume, and he subsequently evaded capture by hiding in a hole in the ground which he had already prepared. Nobunaga's chosen assassin may well have been an Iga man, for we know that he had on his staff five *Iga-mono bugyō*.[10]

Oda Nobunaga's ruthless ways of waging war made him the target of several assassination attempts. Rokkaku Yoshisuke, son of Yoshikata whom we described earlier as using ninja, had seen his territory in Ōmi province invaded by Nobunaga in 1571, so he hired a Koga ninja called Sugitani Zenjūbō, whose particular speciality was sharpshooting with the long-barrelled arquebus. Zenjūbō lay in wait for Nobunaga as he was crossing the Chigusa Pass between Ōmi and Mino provinces, and fired twice, presumably with two separate guns. Both bullets struck home, but were absorbed by Nobunaga's armour and the padded shoulder protectors beneath. Zenjūbō escaped to the mountains, but was apprehended four years later and tortured to death.[11]

The year 1573 witnessed an attempt on Nobunaga's life by a certain Manabe Rokurō, the subject of the 1883 woodblock print by Toyonobu which appears in Plate 15. Manabe Rokurō was the chief steward of a samurai named Fukui, who was in turn vassal of the *daimyō* Hatano Hideharu. Oda Nobunaga destroyed the Hatano in 1573, and Manabe Rokurō was given the task of revenge. He tried to sneak into Nobunaga's castle of Azuchi to stab Nobunaga while he was asleep in his bedroom, but was discovered and captured by two of the guards. He then committed suicide, and his body was displayed in the local market place to discourage any other would-be killers. It is impossible to judge whether or not he was a ninja in the sense of being a professional assassin, but Toyonobu has obviously given him the benefit of the doubt and dressed him appropriately in black.

The American author Andrew Adams claims[12] that Nobunaga survived an assassination attempt at the hands of the semi-legendary ninja Ishikawa Goemon. As so much of the Goemon story is pure fiction it is difficult to assess its authenticity, and Adams gives no source for the anecdote, but it is interesting to note that the method he is credited with using is the one made famous by its use in the 1967 James Bond film *You Only Live Twice*, which for many people in the West was their first introduction to ninja. The ninja hides in the ceiling above the victim's bedroom and drips poison down a thread into the sleeper's mouth.

The most remarkable attempt on Nobunaga's life is recorded in the *Iran-ki* (the chronicle of the ill-fated Iga Rebellion of 1579–81 which is described in detail in Chapter 6).[13] Three ninja each took aim at Nobunaga with large-calibre firearms (perhaps even cannon) when he was inspecting the ruinous state of Iga province that the invasion had brought about. The shots missed their target, but killed seven of Nobunaga's companions.

Other examples include Tokugawa Ieyasu's sending of a ninja called Kirigakure Saizō to murder his rival Toyotomi Hideyoshi. Saizō hid beneath the floor of Hideyoshi's dwelling, and a guard managed to pin him through the arm with the blade of his spear which he had thrust at random through the floorboards. Another ninja, presumably in the service of Hideyoshi, then smoked him out using a primitive flamethrower.[14] Staying with this theme of 'set a ninja to catch a ninja', several popular works mention an attempt by Hajikano Jube'e to kill the famous ninja Momochi Sandayu using a bagful of hungry weasels, though I have not been able to trace the original source. Sandayu apparently thwarted the assassination by the unlikely act of throwing a bag of rat manure over Jube'e, at which the weasels turned their attentions to him, and bit Jube'e to death.

The Noblest Victim
We shall devote the remainder of this chapter to a discussion of what has become the best known, and most bizarre ninja assassination in Japanese history. All popular works on ninja and *ninjutsu* include the gruesome account of how the great *daimyō* Uesugi Kenshin was murdered in his lavatory by a ninja who had concealed himself in the sewage pit, and who thrust a spear or sword up Kenshin's anus at the crucial moment. Kenshin died a few days later. The story, with much detail, appears in Draeger's *Asian Fighting Arts* published in 1969, though no reference is given, and all subsequent re-tellings are clearly taken straight from this book. I have been unable to find any earlier account of it, though a colleague has pointed out that it appears in a martial arts journal published in English and in French in the early 1950s; but how authentic is this story?[15]

Uesugi Kenshin (1530–78) was one of the handful of *daimyō* who survived and prospered through the mid-sixteenth century. His provinces were based around the coast of the Sea of Japan, and reached as far as the Takeda territories in the central mountains. This juxtaposition made them lifelong rivals, and the pair fought no less than five battles in the area of flatlands known as Kawanakajima, where their spheres of influence met. However, by the last few years of his life Kenshin reigned supreme in this part of Japan. Takeda Shingen 'had gone to his White Jade Pavilion' (to use the splendid Japanese metaphor!) in 1573, having received a sniper's bullet during the siege of Noda castle. His death was kept secret for a time, leading to ninja theories about Shingen's death as well as Kenshin's. Their other great rival Oda Nobunaga had blasted the Takeda army to pieces at the

The monk Zenjūbō attempts to kill Nobunaga
Rokkaku Yoshisuke, son of the Rokkaku illustrated in Chapter 3, hired a Koga ninja, who was a monk called Sugitani Zenjūbō, to shoot Oda Nobunaga as he was crossing through Rokkaku territory. Both shots fired missed their target. (From Yehon Toyotomi Kunki, *a romance on the life of Hideyoshi by Ryūsuitei Tanekiyo, illustrated by Kuniyoshi; published between 1857 and 1884; private collection.)*

An actor as Uesugi Kenshin
The most baffling mystery surrounding a supposed ninja assassination concerns the death of the great daimyō *Uesugi Kenshin (1530–78). He died from what appeared to be a stroke while in his lavatory; but his death was so fortunate for his rival Oda Nobunaga that rumours about an assassin began circulating almost immediately. The speculation continues to this day. Here we see Kenshin portrayed by an actor in the film* Kagemusha, *although the scenes containing Kenshin have been cut from the version seen outside Japan. He is wearing the* kesa *(scarf) of a Buddhist monk, and carries a 'rosary'. (Courtesy National Film Archive, London.)*

Battle of Nagashino in 1575, so that by 1578 the Takeda force was a shadow of its former self. Turning to Kenshin's southern flank, peace had been secured with the Hōjō since 1564, when Kenshin, who had remained a celibate Buddhist monk all his life, adopted Hōjō Ujiyasu's son as his heir. So, by 1578, all Kenshin had to fear was Oda Nobunaga, and when Kenshin most obligingly died in the third lunar month of 1578, it is hardly surprising that Nobunaga was thought to have a hand in it. The succeeding months only served to emphasise the benefits to Nobunaga, because Kenshin's nephew and adopted heir fought each other for the inheritance, thus weakening the Uesugi immeasurably.

The actual circumstances surrounding Kenshin's death are quite well recorded, and do not contradict the ninja theory. He appears to have suffered some form of crisis while in his lavatory, and died three days later, during which he uttered not a single word. In a letter dated the twenty-fourth day of the third month to Kojima Rokurōzaemon, Kenshin's heir Kagekatsu wrote: 'An unforeseen bowel complaint [the word used is *mushike*] took hold, and he could not recover. He then lost power.'[16]

The *Kenshin Gunki* also states: '. . . on the 9th day of the 3rd month he had a stomach ache in his toilet. This unfortunately persisted until the 13th day when he died.'[17]

These accounts are corroborated by the diary, the *Tōdaiki*, of a Tokugawa retainer called Matsudaira Tadaaki, which records for the fourth month: 'This spring Kagetora (Kenshin's original given name) is gone aged 49. It is said from a great worm.'[18]

Mushike and the 'great worm' are commonly regarded as the same thing, the condition of apoplexy, or stroke (cerebral haemorrhage). It is therefore more than likely that such an event would leave him incapable of speech.[19]

It is clear, therefore, that something happened to Kenshin while he was squatting over his toilet, and various theories have been suggested as alternatives to the straightforward medical view noted above. The 'ninja theory' – that Kenshin was murdered while in his toilet – whether or not one elaborates on the detail of how the deed was done, is by no means a modern invention, and it is apparent that rumours to that effect began circulating almost immediately. The *Uesugi Kenshin-den* notes that the blame was immediately laid with Nobunaga, who, according to the theory, must have despatched an assassin to stab him.[20]

Sugiura mentions another fascinating theory that Kenshin was murdered not by a ninja, but by an *onryō*, or 'angry ghost'. The notion of an angry ghost was a belief that a person who had died unjustly or by violence could become an *onryō*, and would haunt the living and cause misfortune. The ghost in question was said to have been the unruly and unhappy spirit of Kakizaki Izumi-no-kami Kageie, one of Kenshin's retainers. Kageie was originally one of the heroes of the Uesugi army, having led the vanguard at the fourth Battle of Kawanakajima in 1561, but Kenshin had later believed that Kakizaki was plotting with Nobunaga against him, and had him put to death. He later discovered that Kakizaki was innocent, and bitterly regretted taking his life.[21] The third theory, mentioned by Watanabe, is the most fantastic of all. The fact that Kenshin maintained lifelong celibacy has led certain writers to suggest that Kenshin was in fact a woman, and that the 'great worm', in the *Tōdaiki* account was a complication of pregnancy that led to death![22]

The strongest evidence against death from anything other than natural causes comes from various accounts of the months leading up to Kenshin's death. The distinguished historian Arai Hakuseki draws our attention to a poem composed by Kenshin. He deals

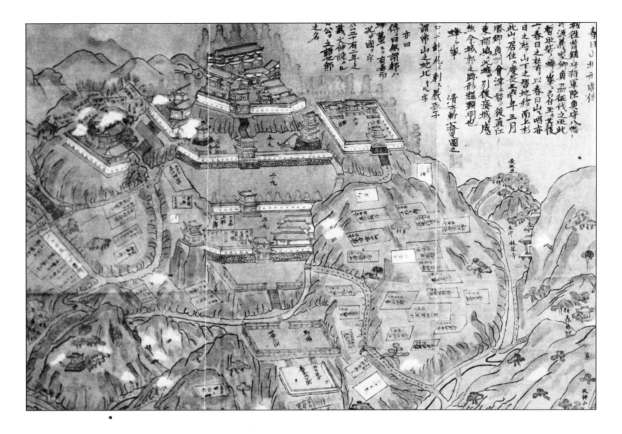

Kasugayama castle
Kasugayama was the residence and headquarters of Uesugi Kenshin, and the scene of his sudden and puzzling death. A popular theory attributes his murder to a ninja who concealed himself beneath Kenshin's lavatory. However, it is widely believed that Kenshin was, in any case, very near to death from oesophageal cancer, and suffered a massive stroke. (Author's collection; from an early map.)

with it as follows, in which he quotes from a contemporary writer, Natsume Sadafusa, who mentions the poem:

At that time he [Kenshin] was angry to hear of Oda Nobunaga's insult to the shogunal family, and therefore decided to destroy Oda Nobunaga and rule his kingdom. It was the 10th month of Tenshō 5, and he would wait until the snow had disappeared, when he planned to go to the capital, and was already gathering his army from all his provinces. The following year in the middle of the 2nd month something happened unexpectedly. On the 13th day of the 3rd month he fell down and died aged 49. According to Natsume when they decided to have the funeral the words of a poem were found under his pillow.[23]

The poem, which the article quotes, is of crucial importance, because it is concerned with his apprehension that his life is coming to an end. In other words in the days leading up to the catastrophe in his toilet he was already anticipating his death, and it was no surprise to him when it came. It is also important to realise that apoplexy may not be so much a cause of death, merely a way of dying, and there is ample evidence to suggest that Kenshin was already very ill when the crisis came. Although normally very fit and active he had had a bout of illness several years earlier which had resulted in one leg becoming shorter than the other, so that he subsequently walked with a stick. He was also a very heavy drinker, and sometime during the ninth month of 1577 held state with

57

several of his closest retainers, to whom Naoe Kanetsugu later confided his fears for their *daimyō*'s condition. Naoe observed that Kenshin had seemed to get more sick as every day went by, and had spoken openly that he himself thought that he had not long to live. So what was wrong with him?

An important clue is given in another diary which noted that in the middle of that winter Uesugi Kenshin was getting very thin, with a pain in his chest 'like an iron ball'. He often vomited his food, and soon was forced to take only cold water, but as a tough old campaigner he surprised everyone by his comparative vitality and his enthusiasm about finally being able to settle scores with Oda Nobunaga. In the eleventh month of 1577, Kakizaki's ghost appeared to him, and it is from this time that the illness became worse.[24]

So the catastrophe that struck him during the third month was not a sudden event, but one that had been obvious to his close associates for some time; all the symptoms point to cancer of the stomach or oesophagus, with the 'iron ball' being the actual tumour. Stomach cancer is still a very common type of death in Japan, and is also associated with heavy drinking. So persistent was the story of Kenshin's 'iron ball' that there was a legend in the Yonezawa area that when he was cremated part of his stomach did not burn. Kenshin was in fact buried not cremated, his body packed in a mixture of salt and cinnabar, but it shows the persistence of the rumour. On the night the event occurred in his lavatory, he had been drinking heavily, and in the lavatory suffered what may well have been a stroke. So instead of gradually fading away Kenshin died suddenly, which is again not an uncommon occurrence among such patients.[25]

The actual details of the supposed ninja assassination with which we began this section are so precise (Draeger's account even names the assassin), that the ninja theory sounds very plausible; but as all the medical evidence points to natural causes, there is no need to look further for an explanation. Sugiura dismisses the notion out of hand, as does the director of Iga-Ueno's Ninja Museum[26] and the staff of the Uesugi Shrine in Yonezawa, where Kenshin's spirit is enshrined.[27] There of course remains one intriguing possibility: that Kenshin was murdered anyway, although it would have been totally unnecessary. The knowledge of his illness would, of course, have been kept a closely guarded secret lest Nobunaga found out, so if a ninja had been despatched it would have been without the knowledge that his victim had only months, or perhaps weeks to live. Kenshin's close retainers knew of the tumour in his stomach, so a sudden crisis may have been recognised by them as a distinct possibility. If this were so, then Nobunaga's ninja may well have unwittingly committed the perfect crime.

6 THE IGA REVOLT

In the accounts examined so far, we have found Iga province to have been somewhat untroubled by the upheavals that were happening in the rest of Japan, and to have benefited from the security of its sturdy mountains to take part in these upheavals on its own mercenary terms. All this changed in 1579, when the men of Iga found themselves forced to fight for their own survival in their own province. The accounts of this obscure but bloody war, none of which have hitherto been translated from Japanese, provide another dimension to the *shinobi* skills of the inhabitants of Iga, because their talents are now used for guerrilla warfare backed up by an efficient intelligence network, as the whole province fights for its own survival.

The Kitabatake Inheritance

The origins of the Iga Revolt relate directly to events in the neighbouring province of Ise, so it is worth spending a little time considering the nature of the relationship that existed between the two. Iga was divided from Ise in AD 680, and rejoined to it in the creation of the present-day Mie prefecture. From early times Ise had always been much more into the mainstream of Japanese life than its little landlocked neighbour. It had a long coastline, the Tōkaidō ran through much of it, and it had common borders with the mighty Oda Nobunaga's provinces of Owari and Mino. It was also the site of the holiest places of Japan, the two Great Shrines of Ise, built in the simplest of styles from bare timber, and by ancient custom (still continued to this day) demolished and rebuilt every 20 years.

The upheaval of the Ōnin War had touched Ise comparatively lightly. As in many parts of Japan the breakdown of shogunal authority was a signal for the Ashikaga's erstwhile *shugo* (governors) to abandon all pretence of ruling by the grace of the *shōgun*, and set themselves up as *daimyō*, so that the territories they governed were theirs, which they defended at the point of the sword. Ise had seen a transition from *shugo* to *sengoku-daimyō* in the persons of the Kitabatake family, a house of glorious pedigree, and it was Kitabatake Tomonori (1528–76) who was to live through the most turbulent times in his family's history. Tomonori was a master of *kenjutsu*, the art of swordfighting, and the pupil of the great master Tsukahara Bokuden.[1]

Iga province at the time was nominally ruled by the Nikki, who, like the Kitabatake, had great respect for the fighting qualities of the men of Iga and gave them little trouble, thus allowing these independent-minded families free rein to sell their *shinobi* talents to less well-ordered parts of Japan.

The challenge to the Kitabatake came from the expansion during the late 1560s of Oda Nobunaga. Since the Battle of Okehazama in 1560 Nobunaga had gone from strength to strength, and in 1568 had ejected from Kyōto the last Ashikaga *shōgun*, Yoshiaki. Nobunaga now ruled virtually as regent, but he was surrounded by enemies such as the Mōri, Takeda and Uesugi, so in 1568/9 his armies invaded Ise to control the important lines of communication that ran through it. Kitabatake Tomonori defended bravely, but lost the castles of Kambe and Kuwana, the latter being on the strategically vital Tōkaidō. Nobunaga then laid siege to Okawachi, and when the siege had lasted for 50 days proposed peace terms. As the chronicle *Seishū Heiran-ki* tells us: 'Lord Nobunaga sent his heir Chasen-maru, aged twelve, attended by Kiboku Shuji-no-suke, to be Tomonori's adopted son, therefore bringing peace.'[2]

Chasen-maru was the boyhood name of Nobunaga's second son Nobuo. The settling of matters by adoption and marriage was nothing remarkable, as we saw in the case of the Tokugawa, and Nobunaga was particularly adept at it. The siege of Okawachi was soon lifted and rewards followed for Nobunaga's generals, who were given lands in Ise – Kitabatake lands, of course. His second in command Takigawa Saburōhei Kazumasu did very well out of it, receiving five districts of Ise as his fief. Kitabatake Tomonori continued to rule Ise as a puppet *daimyō*, in the sad knowledge that when his death occurred the inheritance would pass to Nobunaga's son Nobuo. The *Seishū Heiran-ki*'s account of his eventual end in 1576 is brief and to the point:

Item, in the winter of the Fourth Year of Tenshō, in obedience to Nobunaga . . . the provincial governor's samurai Fujikata Gyōbushō, Nagano Sakyō-no-shin, Takigawa Saburōhei and others went to Mise on the 25th day of the 11th month and plotted to kill Lord Tomonori. What was more, his personal band of retainers had a change of heart. The blade of Lord Tomonori's sword was blunted, and he was taken bound.[3]

It was widely believed in Ise that he was finally murdered by one of his own retainers, a certain Tsuge Saburōza'emon, rather than one of Nobunaga's henchmen.

Oda 'Kitabatake' Nobuo therefore inherited Ise as his own province, but the surviving members of the Kitabatake family did not accept his succession meekly. Tomonori's younger brother Tomoyori had been a priest in Nara, but hearing of what had happened he quit the religious life in search of revenge and gathered the surviving loyal retainers of the Kitabatake about him. Among them, according to legend, was the son of the swordmaster Tsukahara Bokuden. Many supporters also came to join him from Iga, thus bringing the hitherto neglected Iga province into direct conflict with Nobunaga's ambitions for the first time.

Takigawa Saburōhei Kazumasu, Nobunaga's senior commander on the spot, put down the rebellion on behalf of Nobuo, and soon overwhelmed the opposition. Many of the defeated Kitabatake samurai fled to the comparative safety of mountainous Iga, from where they made the dramatic gesture of appealing for help to Nobunaga's deadliest enemy: Mōri Motonari, whose territories occupied much of western Japan and had been largely undisturbed by Nobunaga's expansion. Mōri began a threatening advance eastwards. Matters had now been brought to a head between Nobunaga and the province of Iga, and his son Nobuo was given responsibility for settling the score.

Oda Nobuo's war against the heartland of the ninja has never been covered adequately in English. Our major sources for the campaigns are threefold: the *Seishū Heiran-ki* quoted above, which is concerned largely with Ise and mentions Iga in passing; the *Shinchōkō-ki*, which is a chronicle of the life of Nobunaga, and follows his activities in

Setting out for Ise

The fate of Iga province became linked inextricably with that of Ise when it became the refuge for Ise samurai loyal to the Kitabatake, following Nobunaga's invasion of Ise in 1569. A peace treaty with Kitabatake Tomonori made him adopt Nobunaga's son Nobuo as his heir. The murder of Tomonori in 1576 gave all of Ise to the Oda family. (From Yehon Toyotomi Kunki, *a romance by Ryūsuitei Tanekiyo, illustrated by Kuniyoshi; published between 1857 and 1884; private collection.)*

An assassination

Use of the wakizashi, *the shorter of the pair of swords customarily carried by samurai, to assassinate Kitabatake Tomonori, an act that was to have dire consequences for the people of Iga province. (From* Ehon Taikō-ki, *a romance based on the life of Toyotomi Hideyoshi by Takenouchi Kakusai, and illustrated by Okada Gyokuzan; published in Ōsaka by Kobayashi Rokubei in Kyōwa 2 [1802]; private collection.)*

61

some detail; and most useful of all the *Iran-ki*, written by an unknown author who was probably a monk of Iga, who describes the conduct of the wars against them. It is immensely detailed, showing first hand knowledge of the events and the locations.

The story of the *Iga no Ran*, or 'Iga Revolt' begins properly in 1579 when a disaffected Iga samurai called Shimoyama Kai-no-kami visited Oda Nobuo in Ise to complain about the 'excesses' of his fellow countrymen. This gave Nobuo the pretext and the opportunity for chastising them. Nobuo was well acquainted both with the military reputation of Iga and with its geographical layout (see the map on page 71.) Some years previously his late adoptive father Kitabatake Tomonori had built a castle almost at the centre of Iga on a hill called Maruyama, planning one day to conquer the Iga samurai himself. Such ambitions towards a peaceful neighbour were by no means uncommon, but being aware of their reputation he never attempted it, and the site was abandoned. Nobuo realised that such a base would be essential for his own operations, so he appointed Takigawa Saburōhei as *fushin-bugyō* (building commissioner) with a brief to rebuild Maruyama castle on his behalf.

The Battle of Maruyama

Maruyama was built on a naturally strong position rising some 600 feet (180 metres) over a sharp bend in the Hijiki river. Takigawa did his work well, and the *Iran-ki* tells us that he sent out *shinobi* of his own on reconnaissance missions while the rebuilding went on. However, it was becoming so splendid an edifice that neither the building nor its intended purpose could be kept secret from the inhabitants of Iga. The local samurai families had also taken the precaution of using their traditional talents:

The strength of the castle astounded ear and eye, and in addition *kanchō* [spies] left behind in Matsugashima had become labourers in the castle and spied on it, and were consequently able to make an evaluation of any weak points.[4]

The Iga commanders decided that the time was ripe to launch an attack before the castle was finished, and hopefully destroy the hated Takigawa Saburōhei along with it. The families of Iga rallied round, (the *Iran-ki* lists their names in full), and achieved a complete surprise. Takigawa tried to pull his army together, but was forced to withdraw out of the incomplete defences to the better security of nearby villages. Here they were attacked by more Iga samurai acting in small groups.

A samurai of Hishi village, Ishibe Mijurō, operating in the vicinity of Kowata and Umachō, cut down seven of the enemy even though his left arm was cut off and fell to the ground. Surely he would retreat to the lines? But this strong hero, pre-eminent in this, fought on bravely. . .[5]

Those left in the castle sallied out to help, then pulled back because of the great commotion at their rear. No sooner were they back inside the building site than it was realised that the Iga men 'had techniques for castle entry' so they withdrew again and joined their comrades nearby. It is interesting to note such recognition of a specialist skill being given to the traditional ninja. The fighting went on until dark, as the Iga men, who were familiar with the ground, pursued the Takigawa troops into wooded valleys and flooded rice fields. The victory, a foretaste of what was to come, was almost complete, but note a clever deception on the Takigawa side:

62

Takigawa Kazumasu
Takigawa Saburōhei Kazumasu was Nobunaga's second-in-command during the invasion of Ise, and was given much of the former Kitabatake territory as his own. He acted as field commander for Oda Nobuo during the initial operations to subjugate Iga, basing himself at the half-ruined Maruyama castle. The men of Iga, however, attacked Takigawa before the defences were completed, and sent him back to Ise in full retreat. (From Yehon Toyotomi Kunki, *a romance on the life of Hideyoshi by Ryūsuitei Tanekiyo, illustrated by Kuniyoshi; published between 1857 and 1884; private collection.)*

But the surviving Takigawa soldiers had shown some ingenuity, and when the Iga samurai inspected the bodies they mistook a retainer of comparable build for Kazmasu, whom they thought had been killed in battle . . . so they rejoiced greatly, and raised their voices in the shout of victory. At early dawn the next day they left this place and forced their way into Maruyama, and the keep, the towers, the palace and so on all went up in smoke. They demolished the gates and the walls until nothing remained in any direction.[6]

The truth about Takigawa was soon discovered by the Iga ninja:

Shinobi no mono were sent and when they returned reported that Takigawa had fled away and escaped back to Matsugashima. They expressed great regret that they had failed to kill the enemy general. This was a mortifying situation. And a very sad affair.[7]

The Invasion of Iga
Whatever mortification the Iga samurai may have felt as a result of the intelligence reports brought back by their ninja, it was as nothing compared to the pall of gloom and anger that settled over Matsugashima in Ise when Takigawa's survivors struggled home. Oda Nobuo was for setting out immediately to invade Iga as revenge, even though many of his older retainers advised him against it, reminding him of the fierce reputation of the Iga samurai:

. . . from ancient times the honour of the Iga warriors has delighted in a strong army. Because they are not imbued with ordinary motives they take no notice of death, and are daredevils when they confront enemies. They neither experience failure nor allow for it, which would be an eternal disgrace.[8]

Only the recently chastised Takigawa supported immediate action. He was himself a man of Ise, and had begun life as a Buddhist priest, but had renounced the priesthood to build a hitherto successful military career. To ignore the slight from Iga was unthinkable, and this simple sentiment, so disastrous to generals throughout history, swayed the more rational arguments of the others.

Nobuo envisaged a three-pronged attack on Iga from Ise, using the three main mountain passes that could be conveniently reached from Matsugashima. But spies from Iga once again did their work well, so the men of Iga were able to make preparations, and assembled in three places from which any point of attack could be speedily reinforced. The first attack was led by Oda Nobuo in person through the most northerly of the mountain passes, the Pass of Nagano:

Ten thousand banners fluttered in the autumn breeze, and the sun's rays were reflected off the colours of armour and *sashimono*. On that day he made camp at the post station of Nagano. At early dawn on the 17th day in the steep and gloomy valley of the Nagano Pass his gold umbrella standard came out of the black cloud of the thick morning fog from out of which he pushed forward, as wonderful as the rising of the sun.[9]

He had already divided his army into seven parts to attack the seven villages of Awa, the valley that lay below the pass beside the river that flowed down into Iga. But the Iga samurai were ready for them, and attacked the Ise army in a manner that was to become all too familiar:

They were a strong army because it was their native province, and they skilfully appreciated the advantages offered by the terrain. They had established strongpoints, and fired bows and guns, and taking swords and spears fought shoulder to shoulder. They cornered the enemy and cut them down at the entrance to the rocky valleys. The army of Nobuo were so preoccupied with the attack that they lost direction, and the Iga men, hidden in the Western shadows on the mountain, overwhelmed them easily. Then it began to rain and they could not see the road. The Iga warriors took the opportunity, and, aware of the others lurking in the mountain raised their warcry. The band of provincial samurai, hearing the signal, quickly gathered from all sides and attacked. The Ise samurai were confused in the gloom and dispersed in all directions. They ran and were cut down in the secluded valley or on the steep rocks. They chased them into the muddy rice fields and surrounded them. . . The enemy army collapsed. Some killed each other by mistake. Others committed suicide. It is not known how many thousands were killed.[10]

A similar pattern of successful guerrilla tactics emerged when the second division of the Ise army, under Takigawa, crossed another mountain pass down to the village of Umano. There is some confusion over where the pass was, because the chronicler identifies it as the pass of Nunobiki, which would appear to be much further south. The chronicler also calls it Oniboku-goe – the Pass of the Devil's Carbuncle – which does not appear on modern maps. The Iga warriors watched them from on high, and chose their moment to deliver an attack as devastating as that inflicted upon Nobuo. But there was one particular prize in store within Takigawa's army, for the *shinobi* had discovered that riding with it was Tsuge Saburōza'emon, the former retainer, and alleged murderer of the late Kitabatake Tomonori.

The general Tsuge Saburōza'emon, who was not thought of as capable, was himself pursued and surrounded by spears. Several hundred soldiers flocked round him to take their vengeance, stabbing him together. They stabbed him many times until he died. It was then a misty moonlit night, and seeing the victory won at their hands the Iga samurai withdrew a step back from their violent and furious attack on him. As Tsuge Saburōza'emon was exhausted in body and in mind all need for defence had gone.[11]

The death of a general on the battlefield at the hands of what was virtually a mob was

Killing each other by mistake
The defeat of Oda Nobuo's invading troops in 1579, by the guerrilla fighters of Iga, represents one of the most convincing triumphs of unconventional warfare over traditional samurai tactics in the whole of Japanese history. Trapped by ambushes in the dark valleys that led down into Iga, the samurai of Oda Nubuo fought each other in the confusion. (From Yehon Toyotomi Kunki, *a romance on the life of Hideyoshi by Ryōsuitei Tanekiyo, illustrated by Kuniyoshi; published between 1857 and 1884; private collection.)*

such an unusual and disgraceful occurrence that the killing of Tsuge also receives a mention in the *Shinchōkō-ki* and the *Seishū Heiran-ki*. The former, incidentally, also tells us what Nobunaga was doing while his son was being defeated in Iga:

On the 17th day of the 9th month Kitabatake Chūjō Nobuo went to Iga Province with a number of honourable people. There was a great chastisement there, even as far as a battle, and Tsuge Saburōza'emon was killed in action.
On the 18th day of the 9th month, at the new construction of Nijō, the Regent Kiyohana and Hosokawa Ukyōdayū, amused themselves with football. It was an honourable sight for Prince Nobunaga.[12]

Tsuge's comrade-in-arms, one Hioki Zenryō, fled for his life and returned to Matsugashima, where he was ridiculed by all who had witnessed his shame.

The final third of the army, under Nagano Sakyō Tayū and Akiyama Ukyō Tayū, took a third route which may have been midway between the other two, and could be the same route as today's modern road. They arrived at the village of Iseji, further down the Umano valley than the second army. Here they were met by *shinobi* tactics:

They took on the attacking force at the Jizō-dō, and fought until the sparks flew off them. Both sides raised their warcries as they came together, and fought close at hand. The samurai of the province concealed themselves in various places. The soldiers ran past this group, and then attacked the enemy from the rear. The Ise warriors were greatly surprised by this, finding their return route cut off for them.[13]

Insult was added to injury by the presence in this division of Shimoyama Kai-no-kami, the man of Iga whose invitation to Nobuo to attack had been the useful pretext for rebuilding Maruyama and starting the war in the first place. In this operation he had acted as a rather ineffective guide to Nobuo's army:

Many showed resentment at Shimoyama Kai who had led the attack route. Many people showed on their faces the grudges they bore him. Both Nagano and Akiyama, whose tactics had not worked, joined Shimoyama in his guilty conscience, and barely made it back to Matsugashima to survive until the next time.[14]

The *Seishū Heiran-ki* account sums it all up briefly:

In Tenshō 7th year 9th month an inhabitant of Nabari-gun, Iga Province, Shimoyama Kai no kami, went as an ally of Nobuo-Ason. Nobuo gave approval for him to set out on horseback for Iga. He made his departure and was about to rush in to the attack from two directions, the Nabarigawa, and the Katsura route. At the enemy camp he hesitated, and requested assistance as entering was impossible. Nagano Sakyō advanced and took the place of Shimoyama. He retired from the Nabari route so as not to submit to an enemy grave. At the rear Akiyama Ukon Tayū returned, withdrawing from battle . . . Hioki Daizenryō and Tsuge Saburōza'emon, several times returned to join battle, and at the end Tsuge was surrounded and killed. . . .[15]

Thus ended the second phase of the Iga Revolt, one of the most dramatic triumphs of unconventional warfare over traditional samurai tactics in the whole of Japanese history.

7 DESTRUCTION OF IGA

Oda Nobuo was thus faced with a second personal humiliation at the hands of the warriors of Iga. His mortification was increased by the arrival of a letter from his father Nobunaga. Two versions of its text are reproduced, in the *Shinchōkō-ki* and the *Iran-ki* respectively. The versions are not too dissimilar, and in both Nobunaga criticises his son's error of judgement in going to war the way that he did:

This time it was an error to go to the boundaries of Iga, and an extreme one, terrible even as it would be to the Way of Heaven if the sun and moon were to fall to the earth![1]

The *Shinchōkō-ki* version mentions the death of the general Tsuge Saburōza'emon as being 'unpardonable', and agrees with the *Iran-ki* version that much of the reason for the unfortunate defeat can be put down to 'youthful vigour' on his son's part. The *Iran-ki* text includes some good fatherly advice:

Always follow this suggestion. To break into an enemy's province which is skilfully defended inside and out a strategy should be devised in a secret meeting place. It is essential to get to know the weak points in the enemy's rear. When war is established get *shinobi* or treacherous samurai prepared. This one action alone will gain you a victory.[2]

Two such treacherous samurai (Sun Tzu's *naikan*), presented themselves at Nobunaga's Azuchi castle in the seventh month of Tenshō 9 (1581). Almost two years had passed since the débâcle, during which Nobunaga had been very busy with other matters, but when a certain Fukuchi Iyō, from the village of Upper Tsuge, accompanied by a companion called Mimisu Iyajirō, offered to become Nobunaga's allies and act as guides for another invasion, the chance of revenge for the disaster of 1579 became very clear.

It is evident from the preparations that Nobunaga subsequently made that he considered that Nobuo's incursion of 1579, from one direction only (i.e. Ise), and with little more than 12,000 men, had always been totally insufficient for the job. He envisaged, and was planning, an invasion divided over six different synchronised attack routes, covering the mountain passes from all points of the compass except from that of the impenetrable south. What Fukuchi and Mimisu were offering him was safe conduct on one of the most vital and least easily defended routes, the direct route from Azuchi castle and the north, through Koga, where the mountains were less formidable. The *Iran-ki* also reveals that Nobunaga was originally planning to lead the attack personally, and set off for Iga during the eighth month, the assault having been delayed due to some illness. In fact Nobunaga was struck again by sickness after only half a day on the road. He grew dizzy, and had difficulty with his sight. Sweat was pouring off his body. Being concerned over his condition, the army agreed to return to Azuchi.[3]

By the beginning of the ninth month, he was sufficiently recovered to be able to call a council of war at Azuchi and divide up his army over the various attack routes. The words the *Iran-ki* puts into his mouth sum up Nobunaga's contempt for the Iga 'rabble' who defied every convention of samurai behaviour:

The Iga rebel fellows grow daily more extravagant and presumptuous, aggravating our patience. They make no distinction between high and low, rich or poor, all of whom are part of carrying out this outrageous business. Such behaviour is a mystery to me, for they go so far as to make light of rank, and have no respect for high ranking officials. They practise disobedience, and dishonour both my name and ancient Court and military practices. Because they have rebelled against the government, we find them guilty, and will punish the various families. So let us hurriedly depart for Iga, and bring the punishment to bear.[4]

The arrangements for the invasion are set out below in a table based on the detailed breakdown in the *Iran-ki*. It tallies well with the list given in the *Shinchōkō-ki* and the *Seishū Heiran-ki*, though their summaries are much briefer. It should be read in conjunction with the accompanying map (page 71).

1. The Iseji route
As commander Lord Kitabatake Chūjō Nobuo, and accompanied by Oda Shichibei-no-jō Nobuzumi and Yoshida Gorō Shōyū. This force in excess of 10,000 horsemen.

2. The Tsuge route
Niwa Gorōza'emon Nagahide, Takigawa Sakon Shōgen, Takigawa Yoshidayū, Wakebe Sakyō no Shinjuko, Tōdō Shōgen. This army 12,000 men.

3. The Tamataki route
Gamō Hida-no-kami Shikyō, Wakizaka Jinnai Yasuharu, Yamaoka the *shūkei-gashira* (paymaster). This army in all 7000.

4. Yamato Hase route
Asano Iyabei Nagamasa, Shinjō Suruga-no-kami, Ikoma the *gagaku-kashira*, Mori Iki-no-kami, Toda Danjō Shōshitsu, Sawabara Jirō, Akiyama Sakon Tayū, Yoshino-no-miya Naishōyū. This army 10,000 men.

5. The Kasama route
Tsutsui Junkei, his nephew Tsutsui Shirō Sadatsugu, leading 3000 men.

6. The Tarao route
Hori Kudarō Hidemasa, Tarao Shirōbei Mitsuhiro, with 2300 men.

In all there were 44,300 men. The *Seishō Heiran-ki* adds to its own list the comment:

In the winter of Tenshō 9 an inhabitant of Iga Province called Fukuchi came as ally of Prince Nobunaga and invited in the punitive force. For this reason many generals attacked from all directions.[5]

The *Shinchōkō-ki*, however, makes it clear that the experience with Shimoyama Kai, the ill-fated guide in the 1579 campaign had taught Nobunaga that even these well-recommended 'treacherous samurai' could be Sun Tzu's *yūkan* (double agents), rather than the useful *naikan*: 'Fukuchi of Tsuge was granted clemency, but was taken prisoner and put under guard.'[6]

The Defence of Iga
The Iga inhabitants, whose intelligence service was as reliable as ever, knew that they did not have the resources to ambush successfully six separate armies, each the size of the total they had defeated in 1579. They consequently assembled their main forces in two places for ready dispersal: the Heiraku-ji, a temple on the hill in the middle of Ueno village, which is now the site of Ueno castle, and Tendōyama, close to the site of the ill-fated Maruyama.

Oda Nobuo
Oda Nobuo was an impulsive young man, a failing his father blaimed for his disaster in Iga. Here, he is shown executing three of his loyal retainers simply because his adviser Takigawa Kazumasu had suspected them of treason. (From Yehon Toyotomi Kunki, *a romance on the life of Hideyoshi by Ryūsuitei Tanekiyo, illustrated by Kuniyoshi; published between 1857 and 1884; private collection.)*

The advance of Oda Nobuo is the first to be described in the *Iran-ki* account. He had amalgamated into his army practically all those who had fought with him in the separate smaller armies of 1579, including Takigawa Saburōhei Kazumasu, Nagano Sakyō, and Hioki Daizenryō, who had fled when his comrade Tsuge was murdered by the mob. His attack route was the one that headed for Iseji as used in 1579 by Nagano and Akiyama. The first sentence of the account of their crossing the border shows the difference in tactics from 1579: 'He raided the village of Iseji, and burned people's houses to the ground.'[7]

This scorched earth policy, put into operation by a ruthless and numerically superior army, was the one to be adopted on all six attack routes, with the overall aim being one of forcing the Iga defenders to abandon their villages and take to fortified positions, thus reducing the opportunity for the guerrilla tactics that had worked so well in 1579. Nobuo made camp, having been relatively unhindered in his progress so far. He then divided his army into three parts to attack the surrounding villages and lay siege to the various Iga fortresses into which the rapid advance had forced the provincial samurai. Cooped up in castles to avoid being swamped in their villages their legendary freedom of movement was now of little avail. Ambushes were out of the question. All they could do was mount the occasional raid out of the castles. Takigawa concentrated on the two forts of Tanenama-no-shō and Kunimiyama, while Hioki and Nagano forced their way into the Hijiki valley, where their comrades had been cut to pieces after the Maruyama battle in 1579. Here they burned to the ground a Buddhist foundation called the Kansen-ji:

Many soldiers forced their way in en masse at the point of the sword. They murdered all but one man whom they spared. He was a novice youth called Chōkō, from distant Shimobe. This sad and sacred place which stood there was scoured, and only rubbish adorned it. When the smoke died down, inside and outside were dyed with blood. The corpses of priests and laymen were piled high in the courtyard or lay scattered like strange autumn leaves lying deep of a morning.[8]

Nobuo himself, accompanied by his cousin Oda Nobuzumi, set out for the Ao valley, and the fort of Kashiwao.

A hundred heads were placed in a line of the brave samurai from nearby villages who fought against the enemy. . . . Two inhabitants of Beppu, Arata Kinshichi, Fukumori Kitoheiji and Shirō Hachidayū, put to the sword their ten children and their wives, and set off with light hearts to be killed in action, knowing that their wives and children would have been captured alive and carried off to other provinces. In due time the enemy bore down upon the Jizōdō, a place where in previous years we had chased the Ise samurai away. This time they set fire to it and burned it to the ground, leaving only ashes.[9]

Nobuo's army did not have it all their own way. They may have forced the Iga samurai into castles, but once a siege became prolonged the opportunity arose for the garrison to practise *ninjutsu* techniques on the besiegers. There is a very good illustration of this in the *Iran-ki* account of the siege of Kashiwabara. It is also one of the best pieces of written evidence for specialist ninja skills in Iga, and is reminiscent of the actions of the Hōjō's *rappa*.

The enemy became increasingly careless, including many of the guard outside the castle, and in addition to this from the skilled men of Iga, twenty men who had mastered *shinobi no jutsu*, set fire to various places outside the castle and reconnoitred among the smouldering camp fires. Night after night they made frequent excursions in secret, and made night raids on the camps of all the generals and set fire to them using various tactics. Because of this the enemy became more careful and strengthened the guard. Everyone kept watch, because everyone knew what was going on, so they defended with great caution. Niwa Nagahide's camp was attacked by night on several occasions, and night after night his guards were murdered. Over a hundred men were killed, and because of this the enemy were placed in fear and trembling. Their alertness decreased because they could not rest at all.[10]

Kashiwabara was under the command of a samurai called Takano, who was very good at such operations. On one occasion he ordered a large number of pine torches to be lit and waved about by women and children to give the appearance of a night attack, a stratagem the chronicler proudly notes as having been practised by Kusunoki Masashige.[11]

There is also an interesting account of an incident that involved the army advancing on the Tamataki route through Koga, which shows clearly that the samurai of their ninja

The invasion of Iga
Nobunaga's plans for the 1581 invasion involved six co-ordinated attacks through the mountains of the Iga border. The six routes, and their commanders, are described in more detail in the text. The 1581 tactics had the result of forcing the Iga samurai into fortified places, where their legendary freedom of movement could not be used. All locations have been positively identified – except for Hijiyama, which is not shown on any modern map, though its likely position is inferred from descriptions in the Iran-ki.

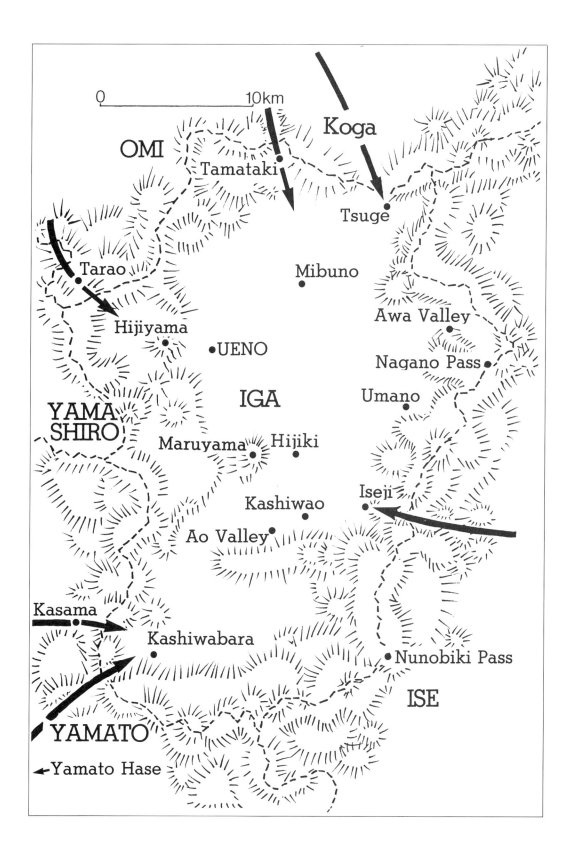

OMI

Koga

Tamataki

Tsuge

Tarao

Mibuno

Hijiyama

Awa Valley

•UENO

Nagano Pass

IGA

Umano

YAMA
SHIRO

Maruyama

Hijiki

Iseji

Kashiwao

Ao Valley

Kasama

Kashiwabara

Nunobiki Pass

ISE

YAMATO

←Yamato Hase

0   10km

neighbour Koga had allied themselves with the men of Iga. The family involved, that of Mochizuki, will be noted later in this book as prominent Koga ninja.

An inhabitant of Koga, Mochizuki Chotarō, was a soldier big and strong, and a hot-blooded warrior. He had a large *tachi*, 4 *shaku* 5 *sun* long, which he brandished crosswise as he fought. He furiously mowed down opponents as he went around with this *tachi*. One person who had fled, an inhabitant of Shimo-tomoda called Yamauchi Zae'mon-dono, seeing this, unsheathed his sword and advanced to meet Chotarō to cross swords with him. Chotarō accepted the challenge, and advanced to kill him. He parried the swordstroke, and then suddenly struck at him and broke both his legs. He killed him without hesitation. He was a splendid master of the Way of the Sword, the model and example of all the samurai in the province.[12]

The Siege of Hijiyama

While this was going on the inhabitants of northwest Iga were facing their own invasion, and had fortified a Buddhist temple called the Kannonji on a mountain known as Hijiyama. The name Hijiyama no longer exists, but it is possible to calculate with quite a degree of accuracy where it must have been, using the names of nearby villages as a guide. It would appear to have been across the river to the west of present-day Ueno city. Gamō Ujisato, who had come in on the Tamataki route, began burning the villages which are now the outlying suburbs of Ueno. Tsutsui Junkei, who had entered from the west, turned north and joined him to lay siege, making his camp on Nagaokayama. The *Iran-ki* devotes several pages to the siege, including several exploits of *shinobi* skill. For example during an attack on the main gate:

Some defended the fort, others prepared an ambush half way up the slope. 1,000 men had gathered. At the Hour of the Snake on the 27th day of the 9th month, both sides gave their warcry. On the enemy side, Gamō, Tsutsui, Wakizaka and Yamaoka were the generals. All the soldiers came in the pitch darkness, suddenly pushed forward and climbed up. The samurai of the fortress skilfully obstructed them, regardless of death. . . . Then the troops in ambush attacked suddenly from halfway down the slope, as the strong army continued to push up the slope. The troops in ambush pushed into them and ran round killing. . . . They shot and thrust, and threw great rocks and great trees from the edge of the ditch. They attacked them with guns fired from loopholes from a distance. The enemy who managed to approach were greatly disconcerted, and many were exhausted. The majority were wounded, and many were lying on the ground.
Momoda Tōbei joined in the victory wielding his *tachi*. He advanced as far as the foot of the mountain, where he caught Gamō Hidesato's two sons. Yokoyama Jinsuke and Momoda continued to advance, confronted the two sons, and took their heads.[13]

Following this tremendous effort, which drove back both besieging armies, the garrison held a council of war, preceded by a traditional ceremony:

Today the reputation of our army binds us all together in joy when we consider the bravery of our soldiers and the quality of the military exploits. The conduct of Momoda Tōbei, Fukukita Shōgen, Mori Shirōza'emon, Machii Kiyobei, Nimi Hiōe, Yokoyama Jinsuke and Yamada Kanshirō have lifted them above the common herd. Due to their talents which are of the highest quality we name them the Seven Spears of Hijiyama here in the 9th month.[14]

But they were obviously not content to rest on their laurels, and the speech continued with an exhortation to use the skills of night raiding for which their province was already famous:

Let us risk a night attack on Nagaokayama and take Junkei's head, which will be amazing to the eyes of the enemy and will add to the glory of the province. If we destroy the vanguard the remnants of the enemy must be defeated in battle.[15]

As may be expected, the planning was meticulous, and we see the name of Hattori, a prominent ninja family, in the vanguard. They launched the attack on the first day of the tenth month, at the signal of the lighting of several pine torches:

The Tsutsui army realised it was a night attack as arrows came from all directions, from up and down. They raised an uproar like a kettle coming to the boil, and as might be expected, in the army many otherwise experienced and brave soldiers had no time to put their armour on and tie it round their waists, they grabbed swords and spears, went down in haste and stood there to fight desperately, combating incessantly. For everyone it was like the month when the gods are away at Izumo Shrine. They could not decide whether to surrender or not and they shed the occasional tear.

The floating clouds suddenly lifted, and an intense mountain wind quickly extinguished many of the pine torches, and friend and foe alike went astray on the dark paths. They could not distinguish between friend and foe in the direction of their arrows, so the samurai of the province made their way by using passwords, while the enemy furiously killed each other by mistake under these confusing circumstances.[16]

But all the *shinobi* techniques in the world would not keep the siege at bay for ever. Successes in other parts of Iga had meant that more units of Nobunaga's army, the Tsuge and Tarao contingents, could now join the siege of Hijiyama. Food was also running low. The *Iran-ki* describes how Nobuo's soldiers surrounded the mountain, and 30,000 troops raised their warcry as they prepared for the final assault on Hijiyama. The shout was met by silence from the grim defenders, every man of whom 'had the appearance of a wooden Buddha'[17] as they stood motionless waiting for the attack. But the final attack on Hijiyama was not to be decided by spear, gun and sword alone. The weather was dry, and a strong wind across the completely surrounded mountain made conditions ideal for the most deadly weapon in the samurai's armoury. Fire would do the work for them, as it had ten years previously when Nobunaga had slaughtered the warrior monks of Mount Hiei in the most notorious operation of his career. It would also be a fitting revenge against the masters of the fire attack:

Ujisato, Hidemasa, Junkei and the rest were greatly chagrined at what had gone before . . . but now they had the means to succeed. They set fire to all the temples over a wide area. This time there was no rain to be blown by the wind. The flames blazed and spread as a sign to the whole world. Some fires were extinguished, but it was many months before the black ashes died away.[18]

The burning of the entire complex of the Hijiyama Kannondō meant the complete collapse of resistance in this part of Iga. Fugitives were cut down or driven back into the flames for an honourable suicide.

As the ashes died down the invading armies struck camp and moved on to tackle other seats of resistance, destroying all who stood against them in a short space of time. The more concise *Shinchōkō-ki* account shows how complete the triumph was, though the dating is at variance with the *Iran-ki*. Note the inclusion of a member of the Hattori family:

9th month 10th day . . . All moved as one through the peaks of Iga Province, and temples throughout the province were completely destroyed by fire. . . . Takigawa and Hori Kudarō rode off on their horses and destroyed more than one of the best samurai. That same day they returned in triumph to the headquarters at the site of the camp.

9th month 11th day . . . Here he took many districts, and punished them with his own hands . . . there follows a record of the heads taken from those killed in various places:

Kobata, father and sons, three persons in all,
the two brothers Takabatake Shirō of Tōdahara,
the keeper of Nishidahara Castle,
the keeper of Yoshihara Castle Yoshiwara Jirō. . .
The keeper of Kawai Castle, Taya, Okamoto,
the father and sons Takaya of the provincial capital
– three persons in all;
Kasuya Kurando, the keeper of Mibuno Castle,
Takenoya Ukon of Araki.

In the attack on Kikyō castle thousands were killed with one sweep of the sword, including the *jōnin* Hattori.
   As for the rest, many were cut down and abandoned at the end. The rest . . . fled to Kasugayama on the Yamato border and scattered. Tsutsui Junkei forced his way through the mountains, inquiring for them and searching for them . . . but the numbers cut down and abandoned are not known. . . .[19]

The Ninja's Revenge

Although all organised resistance had collapsed there was one final act to play in the drama of the Iga Revolt. With the province now successfully pacified Oda Nobunaga was finally able to go and see for himself the land that had caused him so much trouble. The following are a selection of entries from the *Shinchōkō-ki* for the subsequent few days, though once again, the dates are at variance with the *Iran-ki*, which has the campaign lasting much longer:

10th month 9th day . . . In order to have a sight of Iga . . . Prince Nobunaga went up to the Handō-ji, from here he beheld the condition of the interior of the province, then stopped for the night.
10th month 10th day . . . He proceeded to Ichinomiya, and when he arrived, did not sit down even for a momentary rest. Above Ichinomiya was a high mountain called Kunimiyama. Accordingly, he climbed it, and beheld the appearance of the interior of the province.[20]

The account ends on a peaceful note:

10th month 11th day . . . As it rained, his lordship sojourned in that place.
10th month 13th day . . . He returned to Azuchi from Ichinomiya in Iga and entered the castle.
10th month 17th day . . . He presented a hawk to the Chōkōji, dedicated to those who had been cut down in Iga Province. All soldiers had now returned from the war.[21]

The most interesting point about the above paragraphs is what they do not include. The *Shinchōkō-ki* was written by one of Nobunaga's followers, and strangely, but perhaps diplomatically, omits the dramatic incident to which brief reference was made in Chapter 5. The *Iran-ki*, naturally enough, includes it with pride. The attempt occurred at Ichinomiya when Nobunaga paid his visit. Iga may have been devastated, but its spirit was not broken, nor had it proved to be the end of the Iga ninja. Three Iga samurai called Kido, Harada and Jindai, who had fought during the siege of Kashiwabara, lay in wait for the hated Nobunaga who had brought them so much misery. One at least of the three, Kido from Neba village, was skilled in *shinobi* techniques, and as Nobunaga sat surrounded by his followers they attempted to kill Nobunaga by firing three separate cannon at him from different directions. It is a testimony to the ninja skills of Iga that they were able to track Nobunaga's movements and prepare their position in secret. The guns, which may have been the large-calibre variety of arquebus known as 'wall guns' must have been powerful, because although the shots missed Nobunaga himself, they succeeded in

Oda Nobunaga
The scourge of Iga was Oda Nobunaga. He visited the stricken province following his successful invasion, where a dramatic attempt was made on his life by three ninja armed with large-calibre arquebuses, or even possibly cannon. The episode is recorded in the Iran-ki, *and the anonymous chronicler makes the interesting comment that the tradition of ninjutsu in Iga derives from these fine fellows. This modern statue is on the site of Nobunaga's fortress of Kiyosu, most of which has disappeared under the Tokaidō line of the Bullet Train. (Author's collection.)*

killing seven or eight of his retainers. The survivors chased after the ninja with bows and arrows, but being unfamiliar with the area they did not catch them. The anonymous author of the *Iran-ki* concludes this extraordinary anecdote by confirming in a matter-of-fact way the existence at the time he was writing of the great Iga tradition of *ninjutsu*:

Concerning these men, the one called Kido of Neba had acquired strange techniques of espionage and fire. Nowadays there are many people who follow this tradition. They are the *shinobi* of Iga, and they are the successors of these men.[22]

The ninja had indeed fought bravely in defence of their own province, and it was a tradition that they would continue elsewhere for many years to come.

8 SERVING THE SHŌGUN

The spread of *shinobi* activities from Iga to other parts of Japan has often been linked to the devastation of Iga by Nobunaga in 1581. According to this hypothesis a dispersion occurred in which the ninja set up their own schools of *ninjutsu* in provinces of other *daimyō*, who proved only too willing to take them on. The preceding chapters have, I believe, called this theory into question. No doubt some Iga ninja did move away permanently, but, as we have seen, ninja had already been active in many other provinces long before the cataclysm of 1581, and most examples appear to have no connection with Iga at all. However, there is at least one very clear and important link between the destruction of Iga and the use of Iga ninja by a *daimyō*. The *daimyō* is Tokugawa Ieyasu, and his adoption of the Iga-*shū* as his castle guard is the other half of the story begun in Chapter 3, with his hearty approval of the service rendered by the Koga ninja when they helped him twice to defeat the Udono brothers at Kaminojō.

We noted at the end of Chapter 7 that many of the survivors of the 1581 invasion fled to other provinces. Some headed for the remote mountains of Kii, but others made it to Ieyasu's Mikawa province, where they were well treated. There were already considerable links with Iga in Ieyasu's army, as one of Ieyasu's 'Sixteen Generals', Hattori Hanzō, was originally an Iga man, and we noted the death of a Hattori in the *Shinchōkō-ki* account. One may reasonably conclude that several in the Tokugawa army lost relatives or comrades in the invasion.[1]

The corollary to the story is that Ieyasu's benevolence towards the fugitives had an unexpected pay-off the following year. In 1582 Oda Nobunaga, the ruthless conqueror, was murdered by Akechi Mitsuhide, one of his own generals. The attack was totally unexpected, and appears to have taken all of Nobunaga's closest associates completely by surprise. Nobunaga, who was based in Kyōto, had received an urgent request for reinforcements from Toyotomi Hideyoshi who was fighting the Mōri. He had sent on ahead a large contingent, meaning to follow personally the next morning, having spent the night in a temple called the Honnō-ji. Akechi Mitsuhide took advantage of the absence from

An intruder stabbed through the wall
As reward for the service rendered to him by the men of Koga (in 1562) and Iga (in 1582), the future shōgun *Tokugawa Ieyasu took into his service contingents of each, who were to become hereditary palace guards to Edo Castle. Surely nothing better illustrates the foresight of this remarkable man than that he even made the ninja his own! In this book illustration, an intruder receives a fatal and unexpected blow through the interior wall of the house. (From a parody of around 1852 on the life of Taira Kiyomori, with figures by Kunisada and backgrounds by Kunisada II; private collection.)*

Nobunaga's side of his customary large bodyguard, and attacked him with his own contingent of troops as Nobunaga lay asleep. It was far from being a silent ninja raid, with only the element of surprise being present. Nobunaga's small force fought bravely, and Nobunaga himself wielded a spear until an arquebus ball shattered his arm, then retired within the temple hall to commit *seppuku*. Mitsuhide was determined to follow up this easy victory by exterminating all of Nobunaga's family and associates that he could find. Oda Nobuo was far away in the security of Kameyama castle in Ise, but Akechi's men managed to kill Nobunaga's heir Nobutaka in Nijō castle in Kyōto.

Tokugawa Ieyasu, Nobunaga's staunch ally and therefore a potential threat to Akechi, was visiting Sakai when the coup occurred. Having only a handful of personal retainers with him he was in no position to react immediately to Mitsuhide's challenge, and was faced with the difficult prospect of getting back to Mikawa by sea or land without being intercepted by the Akechi troops. The overland route lay via Yamashiro and Iga, where the mountains were infested by bandits as well as Akechi's men. The existence of 'bandits' indicates the presence of an anti-social element in the independence of the mountain samurai of these parts, including Iga, not that this should be at all surprising. In the *Iran-ki* account of the 1579 revolt there are several references to the families of Iga 'burying their differences' in the common good.

With the help of local supporters Ieyasu set off. They crossed the Kizu river (which flows beside Mount Kasagi) with the help of a brushwood boat, which they afterwards destroyed. The *Mikawa Go Fudo-ki* continues the story:

From here on it was mountain roads and precipices as far as Shigaraki, with many mountain bandits. Yamaoka and Hattori accompanied them, defying mountain bandits and *yamabushi* alike . . . Hattori Sadanobu was praised for the great extent of his loyalty, and on leaving he was presented with a *wakizashi* forged by Kunitsugu. On the fifth day Yoshikawa Shūma no suke was pleased to receive a *no-dachi*. Yamaoka, father and son, took their leave beyond the Tomi pass on the Iga border. Wada Hachirō Sadanori accompanied them the whole time . . . and because of the diligence of their faithful service, received a *kanjō* [letter of commendation].[2]

Thus, by a combination of friendly guides they made it to the Iga border. Here more allies took over:

Hattori Hanzō Masashige was an Iga man. Sent on by Tadakatsu, he went ahead as guide to the roads of Iga. The previous year, when Lord Oda had persecuted Iga, he had ordered: 'The samurai of the province must all be killed.' Because of this people fled to the Tokugawa territories of Mikawa and Totomi, where it was ordered that they be shown kindness and consideration. Consequently their relatives were able to pay them back for this kindness. Beginning with Tsuge Sannojō Kiyohiro and his son, 200 or 300 men of Tsuge village, and over 100 Koga samurai under Shima Okashi no suke and others . . . came to serve him . . . and they passed through the middle of the mountains that were the dens of mountain bandits. The 200 or 300 men of Upper Tsuge escorted them through here and then departed. Because Tsuge Sannojō had served in an exceptional way he was particularly praised.

They also performed a service to the community by getting rid of a number of notorious bandits:

. . . Yoshikawa Kiyobei took the head of Ikkihara Genda, and prepared a head-inspection in the village . . . Wada Hachirō and others, who were Koga samurai, went on ahead, and they crossed the mountainous area and lodged in the post station. On the sixth day they arrived at Shiroko beach in Ise.[3]

The serious nature of the perils Ieyasu faced is illustrated by the fate of his retainer

The warrior monks of Negoro
In addition to the men of Iga and Koga, Ieyasu also took into his service a contingent of the sōhei (warrior monks) of Negoro in Kii, destroyed by Toyotomi Hideyoshi in 1585. They formed the basis of the Tokugawa firearms squads of the early Edo Period. Here they are seen in warlike mood, in action against Hideyoshi's troops. (From Yehon Toyotomi Kunki, *a romance on the life of Hideyoshi by Ryūsuitei Tanekiyo, illustrated by Kuniyoshi, published between 1857 and 1884; private collection.)*

Anayama Baisetsu, who took a different route back to Mikawa, and was murdered along the way. Sadler quotes a story in connection with Ieyasu's escape which is almost too good a ninja story to be false! The ship in which Ieyasu fled from Ise was searched by Akechi's men, who had been ordered to be on the lookout for him, so Ieyasu was hidden under the cargo in the hold. The soldiers began thrusting their long-bladed spears into the cargo to find anyone concealed therein. One of the spearblades cut his leg, but Ieyasu responded coolly by taking the headtowel from his forehead and quickly wiping the blade clean of blood before it was withdrawn.[4]

Ieyasu never forgot the debt he owed to the men of Iga, and rewarded them, along with their neighbours from Koga, in an unusual but fitting way by taking 300 of their number into his permanent service. For these men their mercenary days were over, but what vision Ieyasu possessed! The final unifier of Japan, the man whose shogunate was to last until modern times, helped to ensure the domination of his family not by destroying these hereditary corps of assassins, but by welcoming them into his service and thereby denying their expertise to any potential rival. Surely nothing better illustrates the foresight of this man, than that he even made the ninja his own!

The Iga detachment, which was 200 strong, was under the command of the man who appears in popular works as the most famous ninja of all: Hattori Hanzō Masashige, who had acted as a guide through Iga. Hanzō, as he is commonly known, had been born in 1541 as the son of Hattori Yasunaga, a hereditary retainer of the Tokugawa (or Matsudaira as they were then named). He fought his first battle at the age of 16 years in the form of a night attack on the castle of Udo in 1557, and went on to serve with distinction at the battles of Anegawa (1570) and Mikata ga Hara (1572). His nickname was Devil Hanzō, to distinguish him from another prominent Mikawa samurai, Watanabe Hanzō. As noted by Yamaguchi from the *Mikawa Monogatari*: ' Lord Tokugawa's best samurai were Hattori Hanzō, (Devil Hanzō); Watanabe Hanzō, (Spear Hanzō) and Atsumi Gengo (Headslicer Gengo).'[5]

Hattori Hanzō died in 1596 aged 55, and was succeeded by his son Hattori Iwami-no-kami Masanari.

As well as taking some Iga and Koga men under his wing Ieyasu also found employment for a number of the *sōhei* (warrior monks) of Negoro, the Buddhist fanatics whose base Hideyoshi destroyed in 1585. They were particularly skilled with firearms, and Ieyasu took into his service 16 in 1585, and nine more in 1586, placing them under the command of Naruse Masashige. The Negoro-*gumi* formed the basis for the Tokugawa firearms squads of the early Edo period.[6]

Shinobi in the Korea War

By the 1580s, the age of the small, independent *daimyō* was virtually at an end. The petty kingdoms of the 1540s had been swallowed up by a much smaller number of Titans who fought each other on a grand scale, until in 1590 Toyotomi Hideyoshi, the former follower of Oda Nobunaga and the 'Napoleon of Japan', brought the whole of Japan under his control following a series of large-scale and brilliant campaigns that had stretched from one end of the country to the other. Beginning in 1583, when he avenged the murder of his late lord Oda, Hideyoshi invaded the islands of Shikoku and Kyūshū, and made a series of alliances (notably with the Tokugawa) so that he gradually extended his sphere of influence until all the *daimyō* nominally owed allegiance to him. The final campaign of 1590 gave him the Hōjō territories, which he presented to Ieyasu as a reward. Ieyasu chose not to base himself at the Hōjō's main fortress of Odawara but further west, in the small town of Edo. It was a successful move, as Edo is now called Tōkyō, and what is now the palace of the Emperor of Japan was Ieyasu's own Edo castle, guarded by the men of Iga and Koga.

But Hideyoshi was not satisfied merely with ruling Japan. He was now sufficiently experienced in moving large numbers of troops about the country to be able to contemplate an invasion of Korea and a march into China, a grandiose dream he had entertained for many years. His army invaded Korea in 1592, and a unit of Iga *shinobi* was included in the First Division of the Japanese army. This implies that the Iga ninja who had not been taken into permanent service by the Tokugawa had returned to their province and revived their mercenary activities, but there is no record of whether the Korean venture was a paid exercise or not. The expedition set sail in May, led by the enthusiastic general Konishi Yukinaga. From the moment he landed the Korean War became a race for Seoul between him and his arch-rival Katō Kiyomasa, commander of the Second Division. The

The castle of Seoul in Korea
One of the greatest compliments paid to the castle-entering skills of ninja was that a unit of them was taken to Korea during the invasion of 1592. They were instrumental in reducing the fortress of Chigūju, which was the key to the Korean capital. Advancing on Seoul following the fall of Chigūju, the Japanese troops were astounded to find it abandoned, as shown here. (From Ehoh Taikō-ki, *a romance based on the life of Toyotomi Hideyoshi by Takenouchi Kakusai and illustrated by Okada Gyokuzan; published in Ōsaka by Kobayashi Rokubei in Kyōwa 2 [1802].)*

port city of Pusan was the first to fall, followed by Tong-nai, where Yukinaga was the first to climb the bamboo scaling ladders. He and Katō Kiyomasa then set off up the country following entirely separate routes, until they joined forces not far short of Seoul, where the capital was defended by a fortress called (in Japanese) Chigūju. Here Konishi Yukinaga deployed his 'secret weapon'. In the words of the *Taikō-ki*:

The following morning at the Hour of the Ox they advanced secretly to the foot of Chigūju and with one voice shouted in unison. Inside the castle it was as if one was surprised by a thunderbolt. The loopholes were closed and they made ready, and it was every man for himself as they ran about. At this Konishi's army went into the attack. Like a cat cornering a mouse they pursued them, and arrows were fired as they escaped. From within the enemy's great army five or six thousand soldiers returned fire, and defended vigorously with bows and arrows, spears and halberds.

As for Konishi, about half the number of Konishi's hundred Iga ninja had surrounded the castle to the rear and set fire to the castle town, and the enemy began to get confused.

Soldiers who were normally strong retreated along with everyone else, particularly those who had been attacked from the rear, weakened by the surprise from behind against their defences. Seeing this Konishi Yukinaga raised his standard, and his allies shouted.[7]

The Ninja at Sekigahara

The Korean expedition was ultimately unsuccessful, and Toyotomi Hideyoshi died in 1598 in the manner which all dictators dread, that of dying leaving an infant to inherit. Toyotomi Hideyori was only five years old at his accession, and a côterie of jealous *daimyō* began to intrigue among themselves, all eager to be seen as the infant Hideyori's protector. Tokugawa Ieyasu played off one rival against another, until all the *daimyō* were divided into two armed camps between whom matters were resolved in the autumn of 1600 with the cataclysmic Battle of Sekigahara, the largest battle ever fought on Japanese soil.

The preliminary moves to the Battle of Sekigahara consisted of a spate of attacks and sieges on castles, as each of the two rival factions tried to win or maintain a hold on as many as possible of the strategic fortresses along the Tōkaidō and Nakasendō roads. One of the most important of all was the castle of Fushimi to the southeast of Kyōto. It was held for Ieyasu's 'Eastern Army' by the Torii family, who held off the 'Western Army' for as long as they could manage, thus giving Ieyasu's forces time to move into position from the east. The Torii were helped in their defence by the actions of several hundred warriors from Koga, some of whom were inside the castle, while others harassed the besiegers from outside. Ieyasu already had great respect for the men of Koga since their attack on Kaminojō castle in 1562, but the service they rendered at Fushimi surpassed this minor action. About a hundred were killed in the fighting, and after the successful conclusion of the Sekigahara campaign Ieyasu held a memorial service for their spirits. The names of Mochizuki and Arakawa are among those listed that we shall hear of again.

Once Fushimi castle had fallen nothing hindered the two sides from meeting in battle, which they accomplished on the Nakasendō road, the second of the two great highways, and the one which threaded its way through the mountains of central Japan. The Battle of Sekigahara began at dawn of a foggy autumn morning, and was fought for the best part of the day on a restricted front in a narrow piece of flatland between large mountains.

Neither army had established a proper camp, and all positions were fluid, so none of these conditions lent themselves to the employment of ninja. Apart from legends of the famous swordsman family of Yagyū being involved behind the scenes, there is only one account of undercover operations of any sort. Yet this one is quite unique, and was in fact carried out by the Shimazu clan of Satsuma against the Tokugawa.

The province of Satsuma lay at the southernmost tip of the island of Kyūshū, and the Shimazu had therefore enjoyed a high degree of independence from Kyōto and from the *shōgun* for centuries, until conquered by Hideyoshi in 1587. Their territory included the little island of Tanegashima, where in 1542 a group of shipwrecked Portuguese had brought the Japanese their first firearms. The Shimazu were among the first to realise the importance of these new weapons, and among the first to use them, but from 1575 onwards, following Nobunaga's victory at Nagashino, the overall trend had been to use firearms in massed volley firing in field battles. They were also used extensively in siegework.

The Shimazu, however, appear to have developed gunnery in their own individual style of using firearms in guerrilla warfare by snipers and sharpshooters. They had also developed an extraordinary tactic, which Yamaguchi refers to as the unique Satsuma *nimpo* (ninja code), whereby sharpshooters were deliberately left behind when an army

A raid by ninja
This is probably a completely fictitious incident, but it is interesting to note that the assailants have concealed their identity in 'ninja style' and their leader appears to be wearing a fire helmet with a black hood. (From Ehon Taikō-ki, *a romance based on the life of Toyotomi Hideyoshi by Takenouchi Kakusai and illustrated by Okada Gyokuzan; published in Ōsaka by Kobayashi Rokubei in Kyōwa 2 [1802].*

retreated to act, in effect, as human booby traps. The term Yamaguchi uses for this practice is *sutekamari no jutsu* (techniques of lying down and being abandoned).[8]

The best account of the use of these sacrifice troops is found at Sekigahara. The Shimazu fought for Ishida Mitsunari's Western Army against the Tokugawa, and their Satsuma samurai were forced to retreat before the fierce charge of the 'Red Devils' of Ii Naomasa, who dressed all his followers in brilliant red-lacquered armour. On came the Ii samurai, to where a number of 'human boobytraps' were lying in wait. One spotted the general, Ii Naomasa, coming towards him, and fired a bullet which went through the horse's belly and shattered Naomasa's right elbow. Both man and horse collapsed, and Naomasa had to be carried from the field. Within a few months he was dead from the wound.[9]

There is an interesting addition to the story, because the wounded Ii Naomasa received first aid from a ninja in his own service. The ninja was Miura Yo'emon Motosada, who was the *jūshin* (chief vassal) of the Ii. He had first served the ill-fated Imagawa, and Ieyasu had 'presented' him to Ii Naomasa in 1583. *Ninjutsu* seems to have been a family tradition, and when Naomasa was hit Yo'emon gave him some black medicine to drink which was designed to help stop the bleeding. Following the battle Miura was granted a rice stipend of 650 *koku*, which was raised to 824 *koku* in 1608. With Miura there began a tradition of ninja service to the Ii, and their residential quarter in Hikone is remembered today as Iga-machi.[10]

The Siege of Osaka Castle

The victory of Sekigahara was almost totally decisive. Tokugawa Ieyasu was proclaimed *shōgun* in 1603, and reigned from Edo castle with his Iga and Koga men as a secure guard. The Iga-*gumi* duties included guarding the innermost parts of the palace, which were known as the Ō-oku. Here were the quarters of the *shōgun*'s concubines. The Koga *gumi*, who were half the number of their Iga comrades, guarded the great outer gate of the castle called the Ote-*mon*. But in 1614 the *shinobi* were back in action again on the battlefield, when Toyotomi Hideyori, now grown to manhood, gathered into his late father's massive fortress of Osaka tens of thousands of disaffected samurai who had suffered from the Tokugawa seizure of power. Many were desperate *rōnin* who had no master to serve, others were the victims of Sekigahara. The challenge was too great for Ieyasu to ignore, and in the winter of 1614 he laid siege to Osaka's walls, which measured almost 12 miles (20 kilometres) in perimeter. The Tokugawa side used ninja from both Iga and Koga under Hattori Masanari and Yamaoka Kagetsuge respectively, as well as a sharpshooting corps from Suruga, no doubt modelled on the Satsuma example. One of Ieyasu's leading commanders at the siege of Osaka was Ii Naotaka, who had inherited his father's territories and his red-clad samurai army, so it is not surprising to note the name of Miura Yo'emon in his service. According to Yamaguchi, Miura went to the Nabari area of Iga to recruit ninja for use in the siege, who fought in the army as well as carrying out individual operations.[11]

The commander of the Osaka garrison, Sanada Yukimura, also apparently had ninja under his command, but there seems to be no record of how they were used. Sanada had strengthened the outer defences by constructing a barbican out into the moat called the Sanada-maru, and the *Miura-kaki*, quoted by Yamaguchi, records a dawn raid made by the besiegers to capture it. The Sanada-maru raid was carried out on the fourth day of the twelfth month, and led by Ii Naotaka, who crossed the dry moat beneath the barbican's walls. Because there was a dense morning fog the attackers found it difficult to advance, and a hail of bullets came from within the castle. Casualties were mounting as the Ii's comrades galloped forwards and called for a retreat, but because of the noisy mêlée the order was scarcely heard. The ninja leader Miura Yo'emon was currently removing arrowheads from the wounded, and ordered his ninja into action in a move which showed a subtle understanding of the Japanese samurai mind. They approached the mass of men in the moat and fired on them at random. Their comrades, surprised by the arrows that came flying at them from behind, turned towards them and thus 'attacked to safety', the need for an actual retreat having been avoided. Ii Naotaka granted the Iga ninja a *kanjō* for their services.[12]

On another occasion a ten-man ninja unit entered the castle with the aim of creating discord between the commanders in the manner of Sun Tzu's *kan*. We know that one of the commanders did in fact commit suicide around this time, so ninja may have been involved. Both sides also used ninja 'arrow letters', including a secret attempt to bribe

Sanada, which was unsuccessful. The attempt in fact proved counter productive, because Sanada circulated it round the castle as evidence of how desperate the Tokugawa were becoming in their efforts to defeat him.[13]

This first half of the Osaka siege – known as the Winter Campaign of Osaka – came to an end with a spurious peace treaty that led to the flattening of the outer defence works. In the summer of 1615, Ieyasu returned to the fray and laid siege again to the now weakened castle.

Yamaguchi records that the ninja of the Winter Campaign had returned to Iga somewhat dissatisfied with their rewards, and had to be summoned once again by Miura – evidence that even at this late stage those not in service to the Tokugawa were still mercenaries. Here they lent a form of service similar in vein to that of the winter operation. For example, on the seventh day of the fifth month there was an incident at the headquarters of the general Okayama Kansuke. So many camp followers and local people had swarmed into Okayama's camp that observation of the enemy had become impossible, and military operations were severely restricted. Miura applied his ninja version of crowd control by firing randomly into the multitude, who quickly dispersed. There were apparently two or three wounded persons in the unit of Tōdō Takatora, who was nonplussed and in fact praised the ninja for their action. It is not surprising that Tōdō understood ninja, for he had taken part in Nobunaga's Iga invasion of 1581, and had subsequently been granted part of Iga as his fief. Following Tokugawa Ieyasu's recommendation he fortified his territory by erecting Ueno castle on the sight of the temple where the Iga warriors had assembled during the Iga Revolt. Tsu (his former fief) was expendable, advised Ieyasu, 'but Ueno is a treasure'.[14]

The 'Summer Campaign' of Osaka was finally settled by a fierce pitched battle at Tennō-ji to the south of the castle. The ninja fought alongside the regular troops, and Yamaguchi quotes as evidence of their success a record of their involvement:

> Item, one head: Miura Yo'emon
> In the same unit:
> Item, two heads: Shimotani Sanzō
> Item, one head: Okuda Kasa'emon
> Item, one head: Saka Kit'emon.[15]

As the defenders retreated back into the castle from Tennō-ji Ii Naotaka opened up on the keep with a number of very heavy cannon brought from Hikone, and the castle fell. Toyotomi Hideyori committed suicide as Osaka blazed around him.

The Last Ninja Battle

The fall of Osaka castle meant the disappearance of the last major threat to the Tokugawa shogunate that was to arise for the next two and a half centuries. The one serious outbreak of armed strife that occurred during the Tokugawa rule happened in 1638 at Shimabara in Kyūshū, where what began as a peasant farmers' protest developed into a full-scale revolt. The Shimabara Rebellion has always attracted the attention of Western historians because of the overtly Christian nature of much of its motivation. Christianity had been banned in Japan in 1637, after much sporadic persecution. No foreigner was allowed to land in Japan, and no Japanese was allowed to leave. Shimabara thus provided a focus for persecuted Christians as well as rebellious farmers, although the latter had grievance enough. The local *daimyō*, named Matsukura, was evidently an oppressive tyrant, given to punishing those of the lower orders who offended him by dressing them in the straw raincapes worn by farmers and setting fire to the straw.

Matters came to a head when the insurgents fortified themselves in the dilapidated old castle of Hara on the Shimabara peninsula, and defied all local samurai attempts to defeat them. Eventually a full-scale expeditionary force was mounted from the *bakufu*, and the Tokugawa samurai were plunged into a world they thought had gone forever. It is not surprising to see the ninja of Koga returned to their earlier rôles of siege warfare, and the records of their activities, which are quite well detailed, contain some of the best accounts of ninja in action at any time. A good summary comes from a diary kept by a descendant of Ukai Kan'emon:

> **1st month 6th day** . . . They were ordered to reconnoitre the plan of construction of Hara castle, and surveyed the distance from the defensive moat to the *ni no maru*, the depth of the moat, the conditions of roads, the height of the wall, and the shape of the loopholes.
>
> The results were put on a detailed plan by the guard Kanematsu Tadanao, and sent to Edo and presented for inspection by *shōgun* Iemitsu on the 19th day of the 1st month.[16]

A further account of the fighting, the *Amakusa gunki*, gives us yet another synonym for ninja:

> Every night *ongyō no mono* (persons of hidden form) would sneak up to the castle and enter as they so desired.[17]

The Ukai diary describes a particular raid by the Koga men to deprive the garrison of provisions:

> **1st month 21st day** . . . The so-called Hara castle raid was a provisions raid, by the orders of the Commander-in-Chief Matsudaira Nobutsuna. They raided from the Kuroda camp near the Western beach and cooperated in the capture of thirteen bags of provisions which the enemy depended on as a lifeline. This night also they infiltrated the enemy castle and stole secret passwords.

In his account of the provisions raid in his book *The Nobility of Failure*, Ivan Morris mentions the ninja action, but adds the strange detail that they had ropes attached to their legs so that their dead bodies could be pulled back. This seems such an unlikely course of action that I am assuming that Morris has mistranslated the idiomatic expression 'life-line' which appears in the account.[18] The most exciting raid happened six days later, and is recorded in the Ukai diary:

> **1st month 27th day** . . . We dispersed spies who were prepared to die inside Hara castle. Then we raided at midnight from the Hosokawa camp, and those who went on the reconnaissance in force captured an enemy flag, both Arakawa Shichirōbei and Mochizuki Yo'emon met extreme resistance and suffered from their serious wounds for forty days.[19]

The expression that I have translated as 'prepared to die' is *kesshi*, for which an alternative translation would be 'suicide squad'. Yamaguchi adds more detail to the operation. The commander of the Tokugawa force, Matsudaira Nobutsuna, was unsure about the condition of the enemy garrison inside the castle. He suspected that provisions would be running low, so he despatched the ninja inside to gather information. The Koga men were advised that only two or three out of their number could expect to return alive. Volunteers were found in the persons of Mochizuki Yo'emon, whose family name we noted in

A castle escape
The subject matter of this modern print bears considerable resemblance to the description of the escape of the ninja from Hara castle during the Shimabara Rebellion of 1638. In this case, they got away in a hail of arrows and rocks; and they took a Christian banner with them as memento and proof of their exploit. (Courtesy of Jon de Jong of the Oranda-jin Gallery, Netherlands.)

the chapter on the destruction of Iga, Arakawa Shichirōbei, Natsume Shika-no-suke, Yamanaka Jutayū and Tomo Gohei, whose surname appears in the attack on Kaminojō in 1562.

A very noisy diversion was provided by the arquebus squad under Hosokawa, who fired a volley into the open sky, a technique known to *ninjutsu* as 'the hundred cloud gun'. This had the additional intention, which succeeded admirably, of permitting the ninja to attack under cover of darkness, for no sooner had the guns erupted than the defenders immediately doused all the lights, which were customarily provided from pine torches round the perimeter and within the castle. The garrison sentries were of course on full alert, but the ninja concealed themselves in some brushwood and waited until the defenders relaxed their guard later in the night. When it was quiet they scaled the walls using ninja climbing equipment. Arakawa and Mochizuki were first into the castle, but in an act of carelessness surprising to note in ninja, but no doubt helped by the pitch darkness, Arakawa fell into a pit. The moon had risen by the time Mochizuki pulled him out to safety. Yamaguchi notes that both men had dressed identically to that of the garrison forces (no black costume again!), and as the pine torches were rekindled they raced off through the middle of the enemy. To prove to their commander that they had got so far with their mission they tore down one of the many banners bearing a cross that fluttered everywhere in the castle and took it as a souvenir. As they descended the walls they were subjected to a hail of bullets, arrows and stones, which caused injuries from which they suffered for many days.[20]

The long patient blockade of the castle soon paid dividends, and the weakened garrison prepared to receive the final assault:

2nd month 20th day . . . A final counter attack which the enemy had planned was obstinately given back, but now the enemy army that attacked them had only seaweed and grass to eat.

2nd month 24th day . . . More and more general raids were begun, the Koga ninja band under the direct control of Matsudaira Nobutsuna captured the *ni no maru* and the *san no maru*, and after this, until the fall of the castle they were under the command of Suzuki Sankurō Shigenari and his small ten man unit and Nakafusa Mino-no-kami the head of the ninja 'office' sent from the *bakufu*. They had a duty to communicate with the battle lines of each *daimyō* as they went into action.[21]

By the last few days of the siege provisions were indeed low, as the *Amakusa gunki* records:

> White rice 10 *koku*
> Soy beans 3 *koku*
> Miso 10 casks.[12]

As one *koku* was the theoretical amount needed to feed one man for one year, it can be seen how desperate their plight was becoming, and the garrison were down to eating the seaweed they were able to scrape off the rocks at low tide. The commander of Hara castle, Amakusa Shirō, tried a diversionary raid which, though brave, had little effect. It consisted of a disjointed charge into the besieging camps, and served largely to confirm in the Tokugawa soldiers' minds that the garrison were becoming very desperate indeed. When the final attack on Hara was launched, as the diary above indicates, the Koga ninja acted in a liaison capacity between the various units assaulting the castle, as well as taking part in the actual fighting for which *kanjō* were presented.

When Hara castle fell it took with it the hopes of those who had led the Christian rebellion, and marked the last time that ninja would be used in battle. From this time on the operation of ninja would be theoretical rather than practical, with the myth growing stronger the further it diverged from reality.

9 FROM SHINOBI TO SUPERMAN

The Shimabara Rebellion was the last conflict in which the samurai were involved until the Restoration Wars of the mid-nineteenth century, and Japan began what was to develop into two and a half centuries of peace. The Edo period was however no idyll, for it was peace at the price of living under what was virtually a police state. The Iga and Koga units stationed at Edo castle continued to provide the guard as the years went by, and no doubt contributed to the elaborate and extensive intelligence network that the Tokugawa used as one of their means for controlling the *daimyō* and their subjects. It was said of the Tokugawa and their *metsuke*, the 'all-seeing eyes', that everyone had someone watching him, and there is an amusing story in connection with this that relates to the time when Japan was re-establishing contact with Western nations. Lord Elgin arrived as Queen Victoria's envoy, and astounded the *bakufu* officials in that so important an official as he did not appear to have been assigned a *metsuke* to watch his movements. Then one day the mystery was solved. He was observed signing a paper using his full title of 'Elgin and Kincardine'. Here was the explanation. This Kincardine must be Elgin's *metsuke*, and what a brilliant one he was too, to render himself totally invisible!

However, as the stories of ninja accomplishments grew during the Edo Period, merely to make oneself invisible was a very minor skill compared to the achievements of certain of the ninja. Somehow the skilled *shinobi*, whose actual expertise, as we have seen, was impressive enough, became transformed into the black-clad, mystic superman of popular mythology. To some extent this transformation ran in parallel to the other development whereby the samurai, who no longer had to fight battles, became the hero swordsman and the death-defying warrior. But the ninja myth went much further than this, and there appear to be three mechanisms whereby the ninja became larger than life, each of which we shall study in some detail. The first is the attribution of ninja skills to certain historical personages, such as Minamoto Yoshitsune and Kusunoki Masashige, to the extent of crediting them with the founding of schools of *ninjutsu*. The second is to inflate or exaggerate the actual powers of real-life ninja with particular emphasis on skills in martial arts, a trend that began while *ninjutsu* was still being used on the battlefield. The third development is the grafting on to the ninja image of much of the rich Japanese and Chinese tradition of magic and mysticism, so that the distinction between ninja and magician becomes blurred. Add an extra dash of the violence demanded by the mass audiences of modern times, and we have a blueprint for the ninja figure of today, leaping out from cinema screen and comic book.

Ninja in Retrospect

An earlier chapter dealt very thoroughly with the ninja-like aspects of the successful guerilla warfare conducted by Kusunoki Masashige, and his alleged Kusunoki-ryū. For the Yoshitsune-ryū we have to study the latter part of the career of Minamoto Yoshitsune (1154–89), after he had ceased acting as a general, and had become a fugitive. Yoshitsune's last victory over the Taira was the Battle of Dan-no-Ura in 1185, which gave the Minamoto clan a total victory. Dan-no-Ura was a sea battle, and so completely were the Taira overwhelmed that the sea was said to have turned red with the blood of the slain and the dye from the red banners of the defeated army. With Dan-no-Ura appears the first of the elements of mystery to be associated with Yoshitsune, for the spirits of the dead Taira samurai were believed to have entered the crabs that dwelt on the sea shore, and would come again to haunt the victorious Minamoto.

Following Dan-no-Ura, Yoshitsune's brother Yoritomo assumed the reins of power, and was eventually proclaimed *shōgun* in 1192, but in the years between 1185 and 1189 he disowned his brother, forced him to flee, and hunted him ruthlessly throughout Japan. It is this period of wandering that is the basis for the legend of Yoshitsune as a ninja. In Kyōto Yoshitsune thwarted an assassination attempt, and fled successively through Yamato province, the mountains of Yoshino, and finally the remote north of Japan, where he was eventually overwhelmed in battle and committed suicide. His companions on his travels were the giant monk Benkei, and his four loyal retainers, one of whom, Ise Saburō Yoshimori, has on occasions been identified as a ninja. He was apparently a brigand from Kōzuke province, who had fled after committing a murder and joined Yoshitsune. Watatani associates him with the Iga-ryū of *ninjutsu*, and Yamaguchi quotes a number of poems attributed to him.[1]

On one occasion Yoshitsune and his companions disguised themselves as *yamabushi* to escape detection. This part of their journey provides the basis for the famous story of *Benkei at the Barrier*, immortalised in the traditional Japanese theatre. The gatekeeper is very wary of the group, and is not convinced when the apparent leader, Benkei, tries to extract a contribution from him for some pious project. The gatekeeper looks very suspiciously at Yoshitsune, who is disguised as a servant, but when he is about to take a closer look Benkei delivers a heavy clout to the ear of the servant, and berates him for slowing them down. The gatekeeper is therefore convinced that the servant is not Yoshitsune, for no loyal follower would dare to strike his master. Once safely through the obstacle, Benkei begs for forgiveness, which is readily granted. Clearly, there is no magical element in this, but a strange element is later added to the Yoshitsune story in the remarkable legend that he did not die at the Battle of Koromogawa in 1189, but escaped to Mongolia, where he became none other than Genghis Khan. The only explanation for this seems to be that both names are identical when written in Chinese.

A much clearer example of creating ninja from samurai occurs in the Sengoku Period, when the entire family of the Yagyū are supposed to have carried out undercover work. The Yagyū lived very close to the Iga and Koga region, and we noted their presence at the attack on Kasagi in 1541 which is described in the *Tamon In nikki*, but on this occasion they were on the losing side, not the one that used ninja. Yagyū Munenori is supposed to have been used for undercover operations during the Sekigahara campaign. He certainly had his revenues increased considerably (to 3000 *koku*) and there is no record of him

Ise Saburō
*Ise Saburō Yoshimori is an early
example of how an accomplished
samurai could have his
achievements elevated to the
category of* ninjutsu. *He was a
follower of Minamoto Yoshitsune,
and accompanied Yoshitsune on
his wanderings. (From* Bukei
hyakunen isshu; *private collection.)*

fighting in the pitched battle, which has led Sugawara and others to suggest that his service was carried out behind the scenes.[2]

Munenori's son Yagyū Jube'e Mitsuyoshi is the family member around whom have been woven most of the family legends of ninja activities, recounted nowadays in the films and TV series which have been written about him. He is usually represented wearing a patch over one eye, the result of a boyhood punishment from his father, which always gives him a fiercely piratical appearance in his rôles. At the age of 13 years the historical Mitsuyoshi entered the service of the Tokugawa, to whom his father was the teacher of swordsmanship, and began his career as page to the future third Tokugawa *shōgun* Iemitsu. But soon legend takes over from historical fact, and there is one particularly gory tale about his meeting with a Chinese magician.

According to this story Jube'e was then acting as a 'spycatcher' for the Tokugawa *shōgun*. It was in the years leading up to the siege of Osaka, and at the time the remnants of the Toyotomi army were plotting the downfall of the Tokugawa. While doing his rounds near the moat of Edo castle Jube'e saw a ragged man, who was begging for money in a pitiful voice, with his face pressed closely to the ground. On closer observation Jube'e noticed that he had a piece of paper on which he was sketching a plan of the moats. Jube'e challenged him, at which the man screwed up the paper, put it into his mouth and swallowed it. Jube'e, the master swordsman, drew his sword and slashed at the man's abdomen. At this point reality ends and magic takes over, for suddenly the man's intestines flew out of his belly and began to wrap themselves round Jube'e's neck. As Jube'e fell to the ground half-strangled the man announced that he was a famous

Chinese magician called Chin Gen Min. His entrails then completely disappeared. The story ends with Jube'e falling to the floor in supplication and begging the man to join him and come and teach these magic tricks to the *shōgun*.[3]

The main ninja interest with Mitsuyoshi concerns his 'lost years'. The official version was that Mitsuyoshi had committed some error with the *shōgun* while under the influence of drink, but the legend of his wandering starts from the presumption that he was not really banished, but sent out as a ninja, his resulting warrior pilgrimage being the perfect cover.[4] The son of another famous swordsman, Tsukahara Bokuden, is supposed by some to have joined the ninja of Iga when his father's master Kitabatake Tomonori was destroyed by Nobunaga's plotting. Some authorities have him fighting with the Iga ninja during the invasion of 1581.[5] Finally we must also notice a romantic trend in changing a common criminal into a ninja hero. The best example is Ishikawa Goemon, who is an actual historical character. The outline of his life is that he robbed his master at the age of 16 years and killed the three men who tried to arrest him. He then took up the life of an outlaw, but was captured in 1595 and put to death by the extremely painful method of being boiled slowly in oil. Needless to say, he is supposed to have learnt *ninjutsu* (from the Iga-ryū), and appears in the annual procession through the streets of Iga-Ueno.[6]

Creating a Superman

The second trend, that of crediting actual ninja with incredible or otherwise supernatural powers, can be identified in several sources, and what is surprising about this transformation is that it has such a long history, dating back even to the time when ninja were still being used in battle. The description of Fuma (Kazama) Kotarō in the *Hōjō Godai-ki* noted earlier is a case in point. Miura Jōshin's narrative makes him 7 feet (2 metres) tall, among other strange attributes. We also noted that the fear this 'superman' produced among the Takeda was almost paralysing.

Both Yamaguchi and Draeger tell of the skill of another ninja called Kakei Jūzō, who realised that he would be more successful in his practice of the arts of stealth if his potential victims thought he was actually dead! The Tokugawa had sent a ninja of their own to kill Jūzō, who turned out to be an old friend of his. Jūzō persuaded the man to turn double agent and pretended to be captured by him. The man then took Jūzō back to the Tokugawa headquarters. He was brought before Tokugawa Ieyasu, who ordered him to be put to death, but at Jūzō's express request allowed him to commit *seppuku*, which was performed publicly. Jūzō thrust the blade of his *tantō* into his abdomen, and collapsed immediately, bleeding profusely. Well satisfied, Ieyasu had his body thrown into the castle moat. However, it turned out that Jūzō had concealed beneath his garments a recently killed fox, and it was the fox's blood that had been released, not his own. He 'returned from the dead' to plague the Tokugawa for some time to come.[7]

Watatani gives a classic example of inflating a ninja from human to superman, which shows how old is the tradition of embellishment. He is describing the school of *ninjutsu* called the Nakagawa-ryū, which served the *daimyō* Tsugaru who ruled Mutsu province in the mid-seventeenth century. The founder was a samurai of the Tsugaru called Nakagawa Shōshunjin Yoritaka. He was summoned into service by Tsugaru Nobumasa, and from then on he served as an expert in *ninjutsu*. It is recorded that he had a stipend of 200 *koku* of rice a year, which was quite a respectable sum. He was in command of a

土三歳

Yagyū Jūbe'e Mitsuyoshi
Mystery surrounds the life of the swordsman Yagyū Jūbe'e Mitsuyoshi. Heir to a great family tradition of swordsmanship, and close confidant of the third Tokugawa shōgun Iemitsu, Mitsuyoshi suddenly disappeared from public view, officially because of disgrace. However, there are several legends of undercover ninja operations during these lost years, with banishment used merely as a cover. (Photograph from the Ueno Archive.)

group of ten young samurai who studied *ninjutsu* under him, and Watatani notes that he forbade any other men from coming near the place where they practised, which was at the southern corner of the castle. Shōshunjin called the group the *Hayamichi no mono* (the short-cut people) and its numbers increased to twenty. Since the duties of the group members were to act as spies or secret agents, they were to be put into operation entirely on the word of the *daimyō*, and their training was kept strictly secret.[8]

Watatani relates a splendid story about Nakagawa Shōshunjin's first visit to the Tsugaru mansion to be interviewed by Tsugaru Gemban as to his suitability to train the other retainers in *ninjutsu*. Shōshunjin appears to have had a thorough discussion as to his experience and skills, and according to Watatani's re-telling the conversation ended thus:

'By the way, Shōshunjin, when an ignorant person is sleeping on his pillow, would it be possible for someone to use a technique to take the pillow away?'

'Certainly', replies Shōshunjin.

'Try it tonight', says Gemban, 'on me!'

That night Tsugaru Gemban made ready for bed, eager to catch out the famous master of *ninjutsu*. Watatani says that he pretended to be careless, just to make Shōshunjin think that it would be easy. He got on to his *futon* and lay down, and as time passed he heard a passing shower beginning to fall outside the house. He was still awake, and carefully avoided letting his head move from off the pillow as he turned, until he suddenly felt rain falling on to his face. He raised his eyes, and quickly noticed that the ceiling was leaking. In spite of himself his head moved off the pillow at an angle. When he lowered his head once again the pillow was missing, and as he turned his head in surprise he saw Shōshunjin standing beside him, grinning broadly, and with the pillow in his hands!

It is unfortunate that such a good story is probably not authentic, as similar versions are told of other ninja employed by *daimyō*. For example, Watatani tells us that Mōri Motonari's general Sugiwara used a ninja, who according to legend, was asked to steal a sword from his master's bedside, and the famous Tobi ('flying') Katō was asked to steal a *naginata* from beside the bed of Naoe Kanetsugu of the Uesugi family.[9] Yamaguchi adds even more names to the list of those who are supposed to have performed similar feats, of which the one most akin to the above is the story of Sada no Hikoshirō. A samurai called Juzō challenged him to steal his sword:

Juzō returned to his home, shut the doors firmly and the storm doors so that not even an ant could crawl through the crevice, and waited. Hikoshirō came to Juzō's house, he easily cut the wall and entered secretly. Juzō was sleeping with the sword under his pillow. Hikoshirō took a folded paper handkerchief from his pocket and let fall two or three drops of water on to his face. Juzō was surprised and opened his eyes. 'It's raining, and the ceiling's leaking!' he shouted and sat up. Hikoshirō immediately grabbed the sword.[10]

Yamaguchi also adds a variation of the 'test by theft' to the story of the feud within the Maeda *daimyō* household of Kanazawa. Otsuki Denzō, the villain of the piece in the *kabuki* play about the affair (see Turnbull, *Samurai Warlords*) wishes to hire a ninja from Iga called Fukami Kuzō, no doubt to make his villainy more effective. Denzō sets the ninja a test of stealing an *inro* (a small medicine case) from his room while he is asleep.[11] In another section Yamaguchi introduces us to Yamada Hachiemon of the Iga-ryū, who was challenged by a samurai friend to take his sword from him in broad daylight. This Yamada apparently accomplished when his friend was kneeling at prayer in a crowd.[12] One is forced to conclude either that each of these stories is based on one original version, or that the *daimyō* seem to have agreed among themselves on a standardised form of personnel selection!

Swordstealing is however as nothing compared to the other skill attributed to the above Yamada Hachiemon, which is recounted by Hatsumi. Yamada was a master of *semmen-jutsu*, which consisted of giving one's enemy the impression that one had three heads. Yamada had manufactured an ingenious form of ninja headcowl which had a gap at the front for the face, and two dummy heads fastened on behind. This could puzzle an enemy into thinking you were facing in a different direction if conditions were such that visibility was low, such as in fog, or long grass![13]

There are no end of ninja stories exaggerating other human feats. In some the embellishment is relatively modest, such as an unusual form of service noted in the *Kōyō Gunkan*. It was rendered by a ninja called Kumawaka at the Battle of Wari-ga-toge in 1566. The Takeda commander was one of Takeda Shingen's staff officers called Iidomo Hyobū, who seems to have made a remarkably elementary mistake in forgetting to take

Ishikawa Goemon at the Iga Festival
Iga-Ueno holds a ninja festival once a year during which local people parade through the streets dressed in the costumes of the city's most celebrated export. The elaborate float carries a man dressed as the notorious bandit Ishikawa Goemon, who is supposed to have learned ninjutsu *in Iga. (Author's collection.)*

with him the Takeda battle flags, without which it would have proved difficult to control the movements of his army. The 19-year-old Kumawaka volunteered to run back to the Takeda headquarters to fetch them. (One must presume that the direct route was unsuitable for horses.) On arriving he discovered the fortress barred against intruders, so he had to use his ninja skills to climb into his own clan's castle. On another occasion Kumawaka was accused of stealing a manuscript copy of the poetry collection called *Kokon Wakashū* which the Takeda had acquired from the ruin of the Imagawa. To clear his name Kumawaka sought out and found the real culprit.[14]

The *daimyō* of Hirado island, writing in 1821, refers to the ability of ninja to see in the dark, for which they are apparently specially trained; but I shall conclude by repeating the story I used in *The Lone Samurai and the Martial Arts*[15], which is very convincing because it contains no superhuman element at all.

The story concerns a raid by two very skilled ninja. On entering a house they were disturbed by the guards and withdrew. One climbed back over the garden wall, but the other concealed himself in a tree in the garden. When he did not appear for some time his companion became worried about him and re-entered the garden. Creeping up to the tree he called up into the branches, in as loud a whisper as he dared, that the guards had gone and that it was now safe to come down and escape. But the man up the tree, being, naturally, a highly trained and skilful ninja, had had it impressed upon him not to trust voices, lest it be an enemy mimicking the voice of a friend. So he stayed motionless in the branches and ignored his companion's increasingly desperate pleas. The ninja on the ground then noticed to his horror that the guards were starting to stir again, and realised that there was only one way to ensure that his comrade came down from the tree and escaped. He turned towards the house, and shouted at the top of his voice: 'There's a ninja up the tree!' at which point, of course, his companion leapt down to the ground and fled over the garden wall!

PLATE 1 **Treatment with moxa**
Moxa was one of the medicaments used in the practice of kampō *(traditional medicine). Treatment consisted of burning cones of moxa on the body, for reasons akin to acupuncture. (A print by Yoshitoshi (1839–92) from the series Fūzoku Sanjūniso, '32 Aspects of Customs and Manners', 1888; photograph courtesy of Bernard Haase and the Hasegawa Gallery, London.)*

PLATE 2 The ninja as rapist

This book illustration by Hokusai reminds us that the often romanticised and sanitised world of modern ninja myth was, in reality, one of secrecy and savagery. The ninja has broken into the house, tied up the husband (who appears on the following spread in the original book) and then rapes the helpless woman. (From Ehon Futami-gata, *ca 1803; Ravicz collection.)*

PLATE 3 Jiraiya – master of toad magic

Jiraiya was a robber chief who distributed his takings among the poor. He is shown here with his henchmen, riding on a giant toad. (A print by Yoshitoshi from the series Meiyu Suikoden, *published in 1866; photograph courtesy of Gottfried Ruetz.)*

義徹延長尾秋周る
弘沼る股模の姫郷とぬ
く不義は成宝へ含れ
どく多様の悪若え越ひ
懐方女こ成り慣向の展
怕く援せんと弁るその蚤
自ら優なりとぞ

児雷也

玉櫻江芳年筆

松嶋彫政

PLATE 4 The ninja house at Iga-Ueno
Iga-Ueno is the main ninja tourist attraction in Japan. This house was originally the home of the ninja Takakayama Tarōjirō, and was moved to Ueno castle in 1964. It contains many splendid ninja features. (Author's collection.)

PLATE 5 Inside the ninja house at Iga-Ueno
The ninja features of the Iga house are demonstrated to the author by a young lady ninja dressed, somewhat surprisingly, in purple. (Author's collection.)

PLATE 6 A ninja apprehended
Detail from a print by Kunisada showing a guard seizing an intruder who is dressed entirely in black except for a headcowl. (Private collection.)

PLATE 7 The rat becomes Nikki Danjō once again
Nikki Danjō is the ninja magician who appears in the play Meiboku
Sendai Hagi. *In this scene, the loyal retainer Arajishi Otokonosuke
strikes the rat with his fan, trying to make it release from its mouth
the scroll containing the names of the conspirators. The rat gradually
fades away to reveal Nikki Danjō in his true form. (From a print by
Shūnkosai Hokushu showing Matsumoto Koshirō V as Nikki Danjō,
and Nakamura Utaemon III as Otokonosuke; photograph courtesy of
Hendrick Lühl.)*

PLATE 8 Nikki Danjō with the scroll
*The right-hand portion of a print, showing Nikki Danjō with the scroll
of the conspirators in his mouth. (Matsumoto Koshirō V as Nikki
Danjō in a print by Nagakuni, who was a pupil of Urakusai Nagahide;
photograph courtesy of Hendrick Lühl.)*

PLATE 9 Ii Naomasa
The most spectacular achievement of the Satsuma sutekamari *troops
was the shooting down and mortal wounding of Ii Naomasa, one of
the Tokugawa's leading commanders at the Battle of Sekigahara in
1600. This statue of Naomasa is in the Ieyasukan Museum in
Okazaki. (Author's collection.)*

PLATE 10 Human booby traps

The ninja speciality developed by the Shimazu clan of Satsuma was that of highly trained sharpshooters, who would be left behind when the army retreated to bring down an enemy leader as their opponents advanced. This technique was known as sutekamari ni jutsu *('techniques of lying down and being abandoned'). (Author's collection.)*

PLATE 11 The *shōji* stairs at the Myōryū-ji, Kanazawa

The Myōryū-ji is the 'ninja temple' of Kanazawa. It has many hiding places and traps, and is entered by this curious doorway. The steps up to it are faced with paper, as is used on the translucent sliding shōji *screens, so that a guard could thrust his spear through at the legs of anyone trying to enter. The door is also double – and, as it opens, it slides to conceal a secret passage opening to the left. (Author's collection.)*

PLATE 12 The ninja 'Peeping Tom'
In this titillating book illustration by Utamaro, a ninja shines his dark lantern into a bedroom as he slowly draws his sword. The left-hand panel shows a couple making love. (Photograph by the author, from Ehon Takaragura *around 1800; private collection.)*

PLATE 13 Kido Maru (right)
A print by Kuniyoshi (ca 1843) showing Kido Maru learning magic from the tengu. *He is making* mudrā *signs with his fingers. (Private collection.)*

PLATE 14 Revenge of the Soga brothers (overleaf)
In 1193 a hunting party of Yoritomo was disturbed by an assassination as the two Soga brothers, Jūrō and Gorō, took their revenge on one of Yoritomo's favourites, who was the murderer of their father. The revenge of the Soga brothers, admittedly, is more of a classic of vengeance than deception, but the secrecy in which they plotted their revenge, reflected centuries later in the epic story of the Forty-seven Rōnin, *makes it worthy of inclusion here. (From a triptych by Kunisada; private collection.)*

PLATE 15 A ninja tries to murder Nobunaga
Manabe Rokurō was a steward of the Hatano clan, wiped out by Oda Nobunaga. He made his way to Azuchi castle to take revenge on Nobunaga, but was arrested and put to death. (Print by Toyonobu, 1852–86; published in 1883; photograph by Bob Goodwin, courtesy of Philip Roach.)

PLATE 16 Raikō kills the monster of Ōeyama
The legend of Ōeyama is one of the earliest describing disguise and subterfuge. Raikō and his companions disguise themselves as yamabushi, a form of deception later associated with ninja. (From a scroll by the Kano School, seventeenth century, unsigned, ink and colour on paper with splashed gold dust; photograph courtesy of Sotheby and Co.)

英名二十八衆句

花をちの端とむ意文華伊室□店

御所
五郎藏

河竹其水記 [印]

冨士り
准了叡
山嵐み廓の
花の散めくを
雪と都の五條坂
軒と並ぶ遊女屋の
暖簾み曽我の紋尽し
蝶と千鳥の翼加駕牧狩
けろらぬ妹許行渚武者の
士右エ門八仁田の手柄おさ
侠客御所の五郎藏が慥そう
小番七子お燈籠驚たりつき夫
春の末たのから妻のさろ兄の開ま
刑を殺せ一科の腰切ふとそうの息も合
別立尺八のつゆと消行そろ冬八夫婦の縁も
高島の某さく今八記念の偽草紙唯談柄の種

一魁斎
芳年筆
錦盛堂

PLATE 18 Prince Black Spider
The earth spider from Katsurayama is teaching Kurogumo-Ōji the magic of the spiders ready for an assassination attempt. (A print by Yoshitoshi from the series Meiyu Suikoden *and published in 1867; photograph courtesy of Gottfried Ruetz.)*

PLATE 20 The Forty-seven Rōnin as ninja (right)
The left-hand panel of a diptych by Kunisada II (1823–1880), which is an illustration to the kabuki *play* Kanadehon Chūshingura, *a romance based on the story of the Forty-seven Rōnin. It shows two perfect 'ninja', holding a woman captive and shining into her face a dark lantern. This kind of lantern bore a candle on a swivel, and had highly polished inner sides. (Photograph courtesy of Jon de Jong and the Oranda-jin Gallery, the Netherlands.)*

PLATE 19 Uji Tsuneyoshi learns magic
Uji Tsuneyoshi came from Suruga province and learnt magic in Amakusa. His tutor is performing mudrā. *(A print by Yoshitoshi from the series* Meiyu Suikoden *and published in 1866; photograph courtesy of Gottfried Ruetz.)*

PLATE 17 Gosho no Gorozō and the ghostly ninja figure
Yoshitoshi has chosen to pit the hero Gosho no Gorozō against a strange and colossal apparition of a ninja as an illustration to a poem based on the kabuki *drama* Otokodate Gosho no Gorozō. *See the full account on page 138. (From the series* Eimei Nijuhachi shūku *['28 Poems about Heroes'] published in 1866; photograph courtesy of Hendrick Lühl.)*

Plate 21 Tenjiku Tokubei

Tenjiku Tokubei, who lived from 1616–86, was an early Japanese explorer who spent time in both India and Macao. He was alleged to be adept in toad magic, and to have escaped from enemies by turning himself into a toad. In this print by Kunihiro, Onoe Kikogorō III plays Tokubei in the play Kikutsuki Irifune Banashi, *performed in 1820. (Photograph courtesy of Hendrick Lühl.)*

Mail armour

The samurai made very little use of chain mail as armour compared with their contemporaries in Europe. Mail tended to be worn only on sleeves, or as elaborate undergarments on a cloth backing as shown here. Similar suits were worn by police in the Edo Period, and it is often claimed that they were worn by ninja underneath their all-enveloping black costume. (Arashiyama Museum, Kyōto.)

98

10 MARTIAL ARTS

One of the best known characteristics of the superman ninja is his remarkable ability at the martial arts, a belief that was fostered from early in the Edo Period by the formation of several *ryū*, or schools of *ninjutsu*, which had their own rules, their own traditions and their own specialities. The former mercenaries of Iga and Koga, for example, formalised the Iga and Koga *ryū*, and Nakagawa Shōshunjin had his own Nakagawa-ryū. Like all schools of martial arts during the Edo Period they were dedicated to maintaining the traditions and qualities of their craft, and also had their own means of ensuring that the secrets of the art were passed on only from master to pupil or from father to son, with the death penalty for anyone who revealed the secrets to a third party. Yamaguchi quotes interesting proof of this in the form of a *seishi* (written pledge) preserved in the archives of the Ise Shrine. It is from Yamanaka Tōnai, whose name is associated with the ninja families of Koga, and is addressed to Ohara Kazuma, a high-ranking master of *ninjutsu*. My rough translation is as follows, with an attempt to convey the honorific sentiments of the original:

I entreat you to be pleased to accept this which I send you concerning the writings on ninjutsu entrusted to me by your household. They will never be shown to others or told to others outside our company. If by any chance I should disobey then I must receive the punishment of heaven.

Kamanaka Tōnai

Kansei 1st year [1789] 6th month[1]

Yamaguchi also mentions a document called *Shinden ninjutsu hisho* in the possession of the Nishida family of Koga, which contains the phrase 'it is not proper for others to view this without permission'.[2] Both are of quite late date, but are interesting in their similarities to the documents which master swordsmen passed on to their successors. (See Turnbull, *The Lone Samurai and the Martial Arts* for examples).

Many of these ninja secrets were preserved in written form from quite early on in the Edo Period, and as the knowledge contained therein lost its esoteric value in the times of peace some of the manuals were printed as curios. Almost all the ninja lore listed in popular works derives from these remarkable books, of which the best known is the

The headcowl
The wearing of a covering for the head was a practice by no means confined to ninja. Such a garment could provide warmth and a certain degree of anonymity. The latter would be particularly valuable when engaged on a visit to the pleasure quarters of Edo. This print is of the actor Nakamura Ganjirō as Kamiya Jihei in The Double Suicide at Amijima. *(By Kampō Yoshikawa, 1922; courtesy of Christie's, London.)*

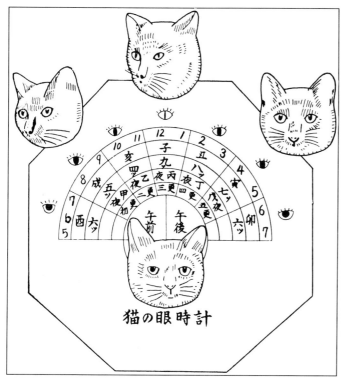

猫の眼時計

The cat clock!
One of the more amusing scraps of 'ninja lore' to be gleaned from books such as Bansen Shūkai *and* Shōnin-ki *is the art of telling the time of day by observing the eyes of a cat. This drawing by Yamaguchi shows how the time may be approximated from early morning (*left*) to evening (*right*).*

Bansen Shūkai of 1676 by Fujibayashi Yasutake, which is illustrated.[3] Another important sourcebook is the *Shōnin-ki* by Fujibayashi Masatake (1681), and Yamaguchi lists 24 others, including manuscripts.[4] The *Bansen Shūkai* and the *Shōnin-ki* provide the material for much of what follows.

The Ninja Martial Artist

The ninja skills of martial arts and the design and use of clever gadgets to further his undercover work made him a fitting opponent for James Bond in the innovative 1967 film *You Only Live Twice*, and have been elaborated in dozens of other movies since, but how authentic are *ninjutsu* techniques and equipment?

To begin with, the black costume: this, the traditional *ninja-yoroi* (ninja armour) consisted of an all-enveloping black garment comprising a jacket, *ko-bakama* trousers, and a hood. According to Hatsumi, the colour was not quite black but had a touch of red. This had a practical as well as a psychological purpose, in that blood would not show if the ninja was wounded, thus reinforcing the image as a superman![5]

One of the most obviously necessary fighting arts of the ninja is the one that is most often ignored in popular accounts, that of disguise. It would seem unlikely that a ninja spent much of his working life dressed from head to foot in black. Most of the accounts of *shinobi* operations which we discussed earlier imply the use of disguise so that the spy or assassin could mingle with his surroundings, an example being the attack on Kaminojō castle in 1562, when it is clearly stated that the raiders dressed identically to the guards. We also noted that a *yamabushi* was a useful identity to adopt, as mentioned above, or even that of a simple farmer would suffice. In Kurosawa's film *Kagemusha* these are the guises adopted by the Oda and Tokugawa agents sent to discover whether or not Takeda Shingen is dead. They wander freely through the streets of the town, unremarkable to any passer-by. Seven recommended disguises are listed in the *Shōnin-ki*.[6] They are:

1 *sarugaku* dancer
2 *rōnin*
3 *komusō* (the flute-playing monks who wore huge basket-like hats),
4 priest
5 *yamabushi*
6 merchant
7 strolling player.

Some disguises lent themselves particularly well to the carrying of concealed weapons. The *yamabushi*'s staff could conceal a spear blade. A rough staff carried by a farmer could have within it a chain weapon. A strolling player's *biwa* could even be a disguised gun, with the match smouldering away in the body of the instrument. The *komusō*'s flute also doubled as a club, but a recent study of the sect includes the comment that such use would lead to a slight mistuning![7]

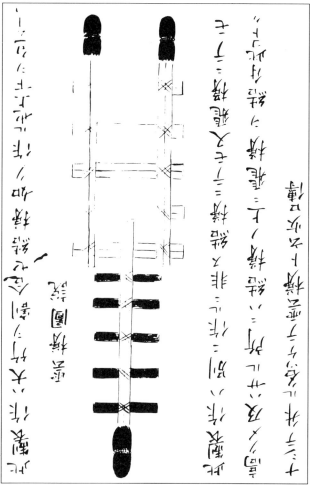

Climbing devices
Bansen Shūkai *is an illustrated manual of 'ninja lore'. This picture from it shows a ladder with a folding strut and padded ends. (Private collection.)*

Among other ninja skills were various ones concerned with survival, such as a useful tip on how to cook rice if you are on campaign and have no cooking pot. Soak the rice and wrap it in leaves or in a cloth bag, then bury it in the ground and light a fire over it. (One recalls Tokugawa Ieyasu's famous recommendation that his footsoldiers should be issued with light iron helmets so that they would receive a degree of protection, and would also have a handy substitute cooking pot.) Sea water, notes the *Bansen Shūkai*, can be purified by boiling it in a unglazed earthenware pot because the salt soaks into the sides.[8]

The growth pattern of tree rings gave the points of the compass, as did the position of stars. A curious feat was the ability to tell the time by observing the eyes of a cat, as in the accompanying illustration. There is also a large section in the *Bansen Shūkai*[9] devoted to the analysis of snoring, the idea being that the ninja could tell how deeply a person was sleeping, whether it was a man or a woman, and most important of all, whether or not the person was faking sleep. Real sleepers were quietly ignored. Someone faking sleep was killed instantly.

The *Bansen Shūkai*[10] prints an interesting ninja code, whereby the *i-ro-ha* syllabary of the Japanese *kana*, in which all Japanese words can be written phonetically, is replaced by a series of complex Chinese characters. There is also a curious means of transmitting simple messages to a general from a mounted scout in a visual manner that would not be understood by anyone spying on the camp. It consisted of making the horse walk in certain prearranged directions.

The ninja would, of course, be as highly skilled as any samurai in the standard martial arts of bow, spear and sword, and the grappling arts of *jūjutsu*, but he would be particularly expert in the field of concealed weaponry, including fearsome-looking *shuko* (knuckledusters). Most of these weapons appear to be genuine. There was also a vast range of *shūriken* available to him, ranging from small knives to tiny darts, as well as the notorious 'ninja stars', the curious, and probably wildly inaccurate throwing weapons spun out of the fingers at a pursuer. Apparently during the filming of *You Only Live Twice*, complaints were laid against the film company by the local council who owned Himeji castle. Himeji was the location of a memorable sequence of ninja in action, and as the castle had recently been expensively restored to its feudal grandeur the authorities were greatly concerned that damage was being done to its woodwork by flying *shūriken*![11]

Tetsu-bishi, or caltrops, were useful little devices to drop when being pursued. Although not a ninja invention (their use is universal and goes back to ancient history), metal spikes that always had one point vertical were a particularly useful hindrance in a culture that wore only straw sandals on its feet. *Kusari-gama*, the sickle with a chain, and various poles with hooks, chains and concealed knives also appeared in the ninja armoury. A strange variety of telescopic spear was also used which could be extended by operating a simple mechanism, but it would appear that this was not used exclusively by ninja.

The Ninja Pharmacopoeia

We noted in an earlier chapter how the ninja Miura Yo'emon gave some 'black medicine' to Ii Naomasa when he was shot in the elbow at Sekigahara. In fact, any ninja desirous of using drugs or herbal remedies had the whole pharmacopoeia of traditional Chinese

Ninja armour?
A suit of lightweight body armour similar to this one is on show in the Iga-Ueno Ninja museum as a ninja armour, the idea being presumably that it was light enough for a ninja *to be able to wear it under his black costume without hampering his movements. (Arashiyama Museum, Kyōto.)*

medicine at his disposal. *Kampō*, (traditional medicine) came to Japan from China during the sixth and seventh centuries AD, but it was not until a certain Tashiro Sanki returned in 1499, from a 12-year visit to China, that its Chinese roots were modified into a form appropriate for Japan. His pupil Manase Dōsan set down his experience in a treatise called *Keitekishū* in 1574, which was the beginning of a really Japanese form of Chinese medicine. *Kampō* consists of careful diagnosis and treatment, with a large number of mainly herbal based drugs.[12]

A very common treatment, which looks strange to modern Western eyes, was that of applying moxa. It was so highly regarded that a samurai was advised to carry moxa with him when on campaign.[13] Moxa is a combustible substance made of the fine hairs densely matted on the undersurface of the leaves of *yomogi* (mugwort, or *Artemis vulgaris* var. *indica*). It is yellow and has no smell. As moxa cones burn on the skin for two or more minutes, a sensation of intense but bearable heat is felt. The places thus to be stimulated are chosen for reasons akin to those of acupuncture, with about 360 therapeutic points distributed over the body. They are arranged in systems, each corresponding to a certain internal organ, and moxa is applied when an illness interrupts the flow of energy through these identifiable points.[14]

A supply of necessary medicines to treat simple injuries and snakebites, etc. was in every ninja's knapsack, according to the *Bansen Shūkai*, which insists that a good ninja could 'live off snow and hail'; but there are various formulae which enabled him to keep going with much less austerity. Yamaguchi reproduces two recipes from the *Bansen Shūkai*; one for pills to stave off thirst, and one for pills to reduce hunger – each a form of 'K rations'.[15] They are appended below in direct translation and are strictly for the historical interest of the reader only (1 *momme* is equivalent to 3.75 grams or about ⅛ ounces.)

> Thirst Pills (quantities in *momme*)
>
> 4 of the flesh of *umeboshi* (pickled plums)
> 1 of *kōrizatō* (crystallized sugar or rock candy)
> 1 of winter wheat.
>
> The mixture is crushed by a stone and made into pills.

For the hunger pills the recipe is more complicated:

> Hunger Pills (quantities in *momme*)
>
> 40 of ginseng
> 80 of buckwheat flower
> 80 of wheat flour
> 80 of mountain potato
> 4 of chickweed
> 40 of *yokui* kernels
> 80 of glutinous rice.

The above ingredients are mixed together and soaked in 3 *shō* (1.8 litres or 3 pints) of *saké* for three years. When the *saké* has all dried up the resulting mixture is rolled into balls the size of a peach. Three should be sufficient for a day's campaigning. The *Bansen Shūkai* also recommends a medicine to resist frostbite in winter. The ninja is supposed to rub *shikimi* oil on to his torso, arms and legs, and according to Kenkyūsha's dictionary *shikimi* is the Japanese star anise (*Illicium religiosum*).[16]

I have been unable to find in the *Bansen Shūkai* any recipes or formulae for poisons, and the ones that appear in modern books about *ninjutsu* are usually attributed to private individuals, if at all; so I do not intend to quote them here. I note from elsewhere the use of human urine as both poison and medicine, the latter particularly by the Priest Ippen, who distributed his urine to his disciples to drink as a cure for blindness and gastric complaints. There is an interesting fourteenth-century scroll painting of nuns collecting the supply in bamboo tubes.[17]

One related aspect examined by Yamaguchi is the use of curses and other written devices. Charms and talismans were customarily written in one's own blood on pieces of paper and carried close to the body. In the accompanying illustration examples are shown of two talismans, and one 'wounding charm', though Yamaguchi says that its use is not clear.[18] The talismans are supposed to have the property of urging a warrior on at

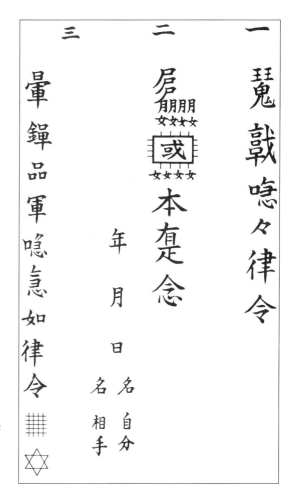

Examples of the talisman
These charms were to be written on paper, preferably in one's own blood, then carried close to the body. The first two (reading from right to left) are lucky charms; the third is a wounding charm, with space to the right for the year, month and day, one's own name, and the name of the victim.

the crucial moment, or to face death in battle bravely. All are associated with the Shingon sect of Buddhism.

The Fantastic Ninja Armoury

Certain ninja devices are less practical than others. In the *Bansen Shūkai* there are various devices for crossing water. The best known are the hilarious 'watershoes', proudly displayed in at least two museums of Japan, which consist of several blocks of wood to be attached to the foot. An alternative has the ninja supposedly walking through water in two enormous pots. Much more realistic is the drawing in the *Bansen Shūkai* of the *shinobi-fune*.[19] This is a collapsible and prefabricated scout boat, which could be dismantled and stored in a box, and could be carried by one man. Yamaguchi states that the Ohara family of Koga possess a model of a *shinobi* boat.

Ninja 'devices' on a bigger scale included a huge battering ram on wheels with a protective roof. These were the great general Katō Kiyomasa's 'tortoise-shell wagons', which were used against fortresses in Korea during the invasions of 1592 and 1598. There is also an alarming form of observation tower which consisted of a box on a rope, hauled up by a pulley, and no doubt hauled down much more quickly once a garrison opened fire on it. Both of these have a genuine historical foundation, but it would be incorrect to conclude this chapter without mentioning certain of the so-called ninja inventions which Hatsumi includes in his book for children. I am convinced that Hatsumi had his tongue firmly in his cheek when he dreamed up these crazy machines, and I am sure he is as amused as I am to see more recent books on *ninjutsu* mention the existence of these as gospel truth without any question as to their authenticity. My favourite, which I include here, is the bovine flamethrower, a wooden cow on wheels from whose mouth comes burning oil. It is shoved into battle by two ninja at the rear. Another is the rotating 'Ferris wheel' for castle attacks, whereby two ladders are joined together by a central hub, supplying an endless stream of giddy ninja on to a castle's walls. There is also a tank, which appears to work in a similar fashion to the bovine flamethrower, and a rather good variation on the battering-ram which is almost identical to a modern wrecking ball. The nice thing about this one is that it would of course work, though stability would have been a problem, because as it was an enemy castle that was being attacked the ball would need to be swung from quite a distance and a great height, so the frame of the machine would probably have had to be unrealistically massive.[20]

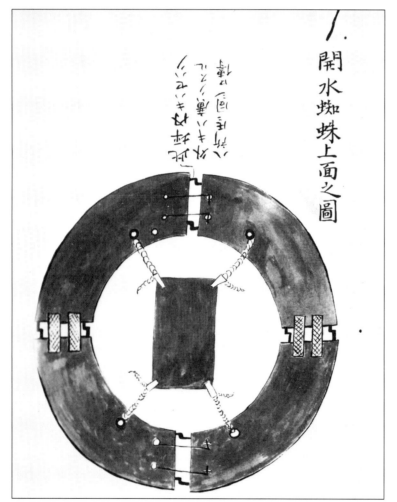

Water shoes
This illustration from Bansen Shūkai shows a design for the curious 'water shoes' supposed to be used for crossing castle moats. (Private collection.)

The tortoise-shell wagons

Katō Kiyomasa's 'tortoise-shell wagons', which were used in Korea, are the sole example of large-scale 'ninja contraptions that did actually exist. Similar vehicles are found in ancient and contemporary Europe. (From Ehon Taikō-ki, a romance based on the life of Toyotomi Hideyoshi by Takenouchi Kakusai, and illustrated by Okada Gyokuzan, published in Ōsaka by Kobayashi Rokubei in Kyōwa 2 [1802].)

Best of all are the devices for naval warfare. There is a submarine, and an 'anti-submarine destroyer' with serrated-edge paddle wheels for sawing the submarine in half! I also rather like the diving gear for ninja frogmen that are like witches' hats from which breathing tubes extend to the surface. Unfortunately, they defy the laws of physics! It is a pity that it all cannot be believed, for then the ninja would have been credited with inventing not only the submarine and the tank but also hang-gliders and parachutes. The Ewok-like gliders were used for dropping bombs. Another form of aerial warfare consists of a plucky detachment of human cannonballs who dropped their bombs while in flight. At this point a parachute is opened, and the human bomber floats safely to the ground over friendly territory, but here I confess that there is one strange device that may just have been true, for in addition to the contraptions mentioned above, there are man-lifting kites. Now the Japanese have always been very good at kite-flying, so it is not beyond the bounds of possibility that one could have been designed that was able to lift a man for a period of observation, and there is one other fascinating piece of circumstantial evidence. In one of the earliest papers ever written about Japanese castles, Garbutt is describing the tower keep of Nagoya castle, which had on top of its roof two magnificent golden dolphins. They were each made of copper and about 8 feet (2.4 metres) high, and heavily plated with gold:

Each of these dolphins is enclosed in a net, which is thus accounted for. A certain robber, Kakinoki Kinsuke, had himself floated into the air at the tail of a large kite such as was anciently used in China and Japan to raise men for purposes of military observation, and he succeeded in stealing some of the golden scales. Whether the tale is true or not, the nets are there, and under the Tokugawa regime the flying of large kites in Owari was prohibited.[21]

Recent movies have added a space-age dimension of machine guns and hand grenades to the ninja's armoury, showing just how far the modern image has moved from the skilled *shinobi* we saw raiding Shimabara castle, armed with hooked grapnels and very little else. (Other aspects of the modern ninja boom are examined in Chapter 13.)

The bovine flamethrower!
The most spectacular of Hatsumi's tongue-in-cheek ninja inventions is this dummy cow on wheels that spurts flame out of its mouth. (Courtesy of Dr Masaaki Hatsumi.)

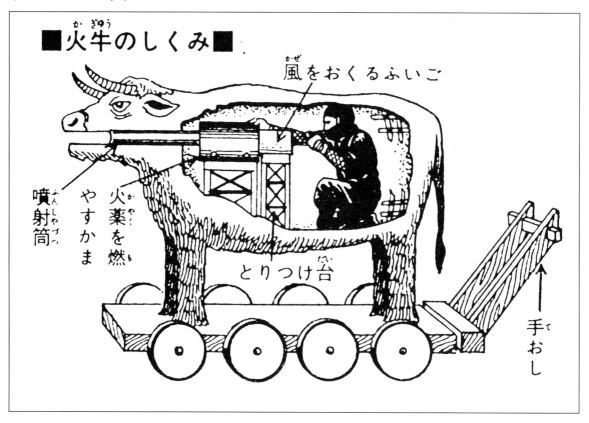

11 MAGICIANS AND MYSTICS

The ninja of popular myth is much more than a superb martial artist. He is a mystic and magician, and once again the tradition of embellishment has a long history. The first very common allusion is to the *yamabushi* (those who lie down in mountains). *Yamabushi*, also known as *shūgensha*, were the followers of the religious sect of Shūgendō, which was a blend of Buddhist and Shintō belief, with a large element of Chinese divination and tantric magic. The *yamabushi*'s speciality was the mountain pilgrimage. *Yamabushi* believed that they could gain certain powers by undertaking these long and arduous journeys, which were accompanied by periods of severe ascetic practices such as fasting, prayer and worship, sutra chanting, magical exercises, and overcoming such discomfort as sitting under a waterfall. The powers which they acquired were religious and magical ones of benefit to mankind, such as the ability to perform exorcisms. They could also see the causes of disease through clairvoyance, and understood the language of birds and animals. With special concentration a *yamabushi* could subdue fire.

Many popular works on ninja make the strange assumption that the traditional founder of Shūgendō, En no Gyōja, was the first ever ninja. Adams is a typical example:

A Yamabushi named En-no Gyoja appeared on the scene and tried to restore order with Shugendo, a new way of propagating Buddhism . . . . Obviously fearing that the yamabushi would gain ruling power, the nobles sent large government forces to subdue them. Forced to fight against great odds, these rugged warrior priests borrowed Chinese military tactics and strategy for use in both individual combat and collective fighting.[1]

There are several mistakes here, quite apart from the completely wrong historical setting. There is the confusion between the mystical *yamabushi* and the belligerent warrior monks (*sōhei*) who formed private armies to defend the interests of the major Buddhist foundations of Nara and Kyōto from about the tenth century AD onwards. En no Gyōja is undoubtedly a historical figure, and Swanson identifies him as a man named En no Ozuno, who is recorded in the *Shoku Nihongi* as having been banished in AD 669 on trumped-up charges of using his powers to control and mislead the people.[2] It is this En no Gyōja who is the originator of the tradition of mountain pilgrimage which, by the Kamakura Period, had become organised as an intensive and deeply symbolic journey which included confession of one's sins from the alarming position of being held over a precipice by a rope round the waist. Other exercises included abstinence from water, and as a man practised these austerities in the mountains he passed through the ten stages of existence envisaged by Buddhism, and emerged from the mountains not only in possession of the mystical powers of the *yamabushi*, but having been 'reborn' and obtained Buddahood within this life.[3]

En no Gyōja was exceptionally honoured by his devotees, and comes over as some-

110

Pilgrims at a waterfall
A print by Kuniyoshi depicting pilgrims bathing under the waterfall on Oyama. (Courtesy of Christie's, N.Y.)

Yamabushi
Ninja are frequently associated with the wandering ascetics known as shūgensha *or* yamabushi. *In this illustration from the* Hōjō Godai-ki, *a samurai – identified as such by his possession of a bow and quiver – is making a purchase, possibly some medicament, from a passing* yamabushi. *(From a woodblock-printed edition of the* Hōjō Godai-ki *[1659]; private collection.)*

En no Gyōja
This statue of En no Gyōja ('En the Ascetic') is on the summit of Mount Ōmine. En no Gyōja is often incorrectly named as the founder of ninjutsu. In fact, he was the originator of the tradition of mountain pilgrimage. (Author's collection.)

thing of a demonic figure. But he is not a hired assassin or a guerrilla fighter, and on the face of it ninja and *yamabushi* seem to have little in common apart from their inherent mystery. Perhaps one reason for this association may well be that the guise of a wandering *yamabushi* was the ideal cover for a rôle that involved espionage and travel. As we noted earlier, one of the greatest legends of Japan, that of Benkei and Yoshitsune's flight from Yoritomo, has them disguised as *yamabushi* in the famous scene at the barrier, where the fugitives are challenged about their real identity. Rotermund goes further, and states that *yamabushi* themselves acted as spies for rival *daimyō*, thereby abusing their right of free travel.[4]

However, I think there is more to it than that. First, the area particularly associated with ninja activity, namely the Iga area, is very close to important places associated both with undercover resistance (such as Kasagi and Yoshino), and also *yamabushi*. The Iga mountains reach into the Yoshino range, and loom over that vital artery of the Tōkaidō as it begins its curve inland towards Kyōto and away from the comforting backdrop of the sea. The mountains of this area, the Kii Peninsula, can still be very wild in nature today, as the author may confirm from personal experience. It is associated with the figures of Yoshitsune and Masashige, and is also crossed by the traditional route of *yamabushi* pilgrimages and their associated rituals, of which the most important journey was from

112

The mountain pilgrimage
Travellers on a pilgrimage on Mount Fuji complete their journey in this print by Hokusai. (From Hokusai's Thirty-Six Views of Mount Fuji, *Courtesy of Christie's, N.Y.)*

Yoshino to Kumano. In the villages hidden deep in the mountains lived communities shut off from the rest of Japan until comparatively recent times. So on one hand you have the ninja of Iga and Koga hiring out their skills to rival *daimyō*, plus romantic legends of fugitive emperors and samurai, and on the other there are the esoteric mysteries of Shūgendō, whose *yamabushi* were probably the only outsiders for centuries to venture into these mountains. One therefore has the perfect ingredients of military skill, romance and mystery ready to be blended into the figure of the ninja, with *yamabushi* supplying much of the esoteric side.

There may also be one other factor involved in building up the mystic ninja image. This factor is the legend of the *tengu*, the little goblins, half-man and half-crow, whose swordfighting skills were legendary. De Visser tells us that during the Kamakura Period the notion of *tengu* became associated with *yamabushi*, so that it was thought either that *tengu* took the form of *yamabushi*, or temporarily possessed them.[5] As to their military skills, by tradition it was the *tengu* who taught Yoshitsune the arts of swordfighting when he was a novice monk on Mount Kurama. Furthermore, in later works of art the *tengu* are almost invariably represented as *yamabushi*, as illustrated by the remarkable suit of armour preserved in the Arishiyama Museum in Kyōto. Joly distinguishes between the bird-like *karasu-tengu* and the more human-like *konoha-tengu* who has wings and a very

113

long nose. It is the *konoha-tengu*, according to Joly, who in the forests goes along clad only in leaves, but 'shows himself among men in the guise of a *yamabushi*.'[6] He also mentions the swordfighting, and adds that the famous Miyamoto Musashi defeated and killed a *tengu* in combat. It is not a great leap of imagination to link the swordfighting *tengu* with gangs of bandits operating in forested mountains, and later hiring their skills to others as ninja, so it may well be that part at least of the mysterious side of ninja lore is based on *tengu*.

The Ninja and Magic

We may therefore conclude, not unreasonably, that the ninja of popular myth has acquired something of the spiritual power of the *yamabushi* and the merry wilfulness of *tengu*. All that requires to be added is some measure of magic. *Yamabushi* may have had their own magic, but they were after all only human, and if one were to combine the ninja's military skills with the rich legend of Chinese and Japanese magicians the resulting combination of superhero and mystic would be almost limitless in its powers. We noted in the previous chapter the sword-stealing expertise of Nakagawa Shōshunjin. One account of his life, which Watatani quotes, is the *Okufuji monogatari*, which includes in its description of him the fascinating phrase: '. . . moreover, he could change into a rat or a spider, and transform himself into birds and animals'. This is as neat an illustration of the fantastic power attributed to ninja as one is likely to find at any time.

It is not difficult to see possible sources for the magical powers of ninja, because magic appears everywhere in Japanese history. We noted Prince Morinaga using invisibility spells to hide from his pursuers, and Murdoch, writing of the Emperor Shōkō (1412–28) a century later, observes drily:

The Sovereign was greatly addicted to the study and practice of magic arts, in which it was believed that proficiency could not be attained without the strictest observation of continence, and he died without children.[8]

Apart from emperors and princes there are a number of individual magicians who are linked to ninja-like activities such as revenge attacks and spying. Many are associated with robber gangs in mountains, or with *tengu*. Kurogumo-oji, 'Prince Black Spider', learned spider magic to prepare himself for an assassination. Inuyama Tadaoki learned fire magic so that he could avenge his father. Tengu-kozo Kiritarō was a robber chief who, like Yoshitsune, learned magic from the *tengu*. Madara-maru was another robber who used magic. Shimazu Yoshitaka, a retainer of Kiso Yoshinaka, used magic in an attempt to kill Yoritomo, and so on.

Chinese mythology adds its own vein of richness. From this quarter are borrowed the stories of the *sennin*, or mountain men, immortals who have reached that stage by prolonged practice of similar rites in mountains to those mentioned above in connection

Yoshitsune and the *tengu*
The tengu, *the mythical goblins – who were half-man and half-crow – may well provide some of the elements which go to make up the composite figure of the ninja of today. In this print by Kuniyoshi (about 1850), the young Minamoto Yoshitsune is being taught the tricks of swordfighting by the* tengu *of Mount Kurama. (Private collection.)*

with *yamabushi*. But unlike a *yamabushi* whose pilgrimage takes him through the mountains to return, to a *sennin* the mountain is his home. They are usually depicted in art as old sage-like men with long beards, and all have magical powers. Gama Sennin ('the *sennin* of the toad'), for example, was an adept at toad magic. He is also referred to as Kosensei. He had no hair, and his body was covered in protuberances like a toad's skin. Kosensei put his magical powers to practical use by selling drugs endowed with magical powers. He is usually depicted in art accompanied by a toad, which is sometimes as big as he is, in a similar style to Tenjiku Tobukei who his shown in one of the colour plates. Tenjiku Tokubei was not a *sennin*, but an historical character who lived from 1618–86, and was an early explorer of foreign countries in the years prior to the seclusion order. He spent three years in India and two in Macao. Legend has credited him with the skills of *ninjutsu*, and he is often depicted riding on a giant toad. Another toad magician is Jiraiya, otherwise known as Ogata Hiroyuki, who was a robber baron who distributed his goods among the poor. Once again we see an association between a robber chief and magic.

Other *sennin* are associated with different forms of magic, such as the control of fire. Yoko Sennin was able to destroy his own shadow, divide his own body, and live in the midst of flames. A certain King, to try him, had him burnt on a pile of brushwood. When the flames subsided Yoko was seen squatting in the ashes, and unconcernedly reading a book. One *sennin*, Oshikyo, knew secrets of longevity, and left for the use of later generations the following formula, quoted in Joly:

Gather from a chrysanthemum the young shoots on the day of the tiger in the third month, leaves in the sixth, the flowers in the ninth and the remaining stem and root during the twelfth month. Dry separately in the shade; pulverise on the day of the dog equal parts of each. Make into pills with honey, or mix with wine, one *momme* of the powder and take daily three times, each dose being divided into seven parts the size of a small seed. After a hundred days the body will become lighter, the white hair will blacken in a year, and in ten years new teeth will have grown, and after five years' steady absorption of this nostrum an old man of eighty will feel young, his skin will be supple and fair, and he will never age again.[9]

Other recipes for longevity include sesame seed porridge, sulphur, potash and cinnabar, though Joly adds:

We are told of several cases when the use of the elixir resulted in apparently sudden death, but the disciples always beheld the holy user among the genii immediately after the absorption of the drug. In the case of Wei Peh Yang, the wizard tried the stuff on his dog, who died.[10]

Ninja Finger-signs

One of the best known of ninja magic tricks involves strange signs made by the fingers. The signs consist of various combinations of different gestures made by knotting the fingers together. The characters for the signs can also be written down in a three-by-three grid. Claims have been made that they were used by a ninja to hypnotise an enemy into inaction, or to give the ninja a sudden surge in power, but their origin is somewhat different.

The signs are actually examples of *mudrā*, a Sanskrit word meaning, quite simply, gestures made with the hands. They are particularly noticeable on Buddhist statues, and were introduced into Japan in the seventh century AD by the monk Kōbō Daishi, founder of the Shingon sect of esoteric Buddhism. In Kōbō Daishi's formulation *mudrā* involved a manipulation of the fingers to supplement the power of words, and a Shingon manual,

Armour styled as a *tengu*
This remarkable suit of armour is modelled to represent a tengu. *Note the crow's beak above the facemask, and in particular the pill-box hat of a* yamabushi. Tengu *were believed to assume the form of a* yamabushi *in order to play pranks on humans. (Courtesy of Arashiyama Museum, Kyoto.)*

Initiation
This dramatic print by Yoshitoshi represents initiation. The novice, praying before a statue of Fudō, dreams that the statue comes to life and pierces him with the sword. (Courtesy of Christie's, London.)

quoted by Saunders, lists 295 different ones, some of which were performed by a priest as part of a ritual, while others appeared on statues.[11] Every arrangement of the fingers has a particular significance, and every part of each hand has its own meaning when touched by a finger, making one's hands into a form of 'rosary'. They are therefore most closely associated with the religious rituals of Shingon Buddhism, but historically have often been granted a magical component. As an example of this we may note the use of magical *mudrā* by an opponent of Sugawara Michizane (AD 845–903), as recounted in the *Taiheiki*, where the life of Michizane (here referred to as the 'Kan minister of state') is recalled to illustrate a point the writer is making:

Then suddenly the face of the Kan minister of state grew wroth. He took up a pomegranate from before him, crunched it with his teeth, and spat it out against the door of the hall. And the seeds became a violent fire, burning the door. Yet the monk reformer was in no way affrighted, but turned his face towards the burning fire, made the water-sprinkling sign with his hands, and extinguished the fierce flames in an instant.[12]

It is also quite common to see magicians depicted in works of art making these gestures with their fingers. For example in the print of Inuyama Tadaoki, the master of fire magic, we note the combination of a 'diamond fist' with a 'lotus fist' to make a 'Tathagata fist', as identified in Saunders' book. (Note also Plate 7, of Nikki Danjō being transformed back from a rat.) The bizarre-looking magician tutor, who looms up behind Uji Tsuneyoshi in the plate depicting his magic lessons, is making an unusual gesture which appears to combine two 'anger fists' in one, which is not unlike the one adopted by Kido maru in Plate 13 showing him learning magic from the *tengu*.

In conclusion, the finger signs are firmly rooted in Buddhist ritual practice and have a very long history of being associated with magic. Their use by martial arts practitioners may have arisen as a result of certain *sensei* belonging to the Shingon sect where such rituals are commonplace, but its purpose is a little unclear. Its widespread use today by modern students of *ninjutsu* provides a curious link with the past, but one that I feel is somewhat misplaced.

Tobi Katō – Ninja Magician

It has been difficult to choose an example of a legend of ninja magic because the dividing line is very fine between the ninja as superman and the ninja as a magician, and several stories related in the previous chapter have a magical side to them. But there is one ninja indeed to whom were credited magical properties in addition to his ninja skills. This was Katō Danjō, nicknamed Tobi Katō ('Flying Katō'). He was born in Hitachi province, and came to the attention of Uesugi Kenshin. According to Yamaguchi's telling of the story Tobi Katō used his magical skills to amaze and frighten the townspeople. On one occasion he quelled a fierce bull that was running wild. At another time he used magical skills that look suspiciously like conjuring tricks. He took two leaves from a sapling that was growing in the grass, and waved at them vigorously with his fan. To the amazement of all the leaves took root and sprouted, and very soon there was a full-sized tree from

Ishikawa Goemon performs *mudrā*
Ishikawa Goemon is disguised as a farmer called Gosaku. He clasps his fingers together in a mudrā *to summon up ghostly warriors. The actor Nakamura Utaemon is playing the role of Goemon in this print by Shunkōsai Hokushū of 1830. (Private collection.)*

whose branches hung bottle-gourds. To prove the tree was genuine Tobi Katō took his sword and cut off one of the gourds for the crowd's inspection.

Such antics came to the ear of Uesugi Kenshin, who realised that Tobi Katō may be worth hiring as a ninja. However, he first decided to test Katō a little further. The test chosen was (unsurprisingly!) to steal a weapon, in this case a *naginata*, from the bedside of his retainer Naoe Kanetsugu. His mission was little more difficult than the examples mentioned in the previous chapter, for the Naoe house was large one, and guarded by a very fierce dog called Murasame. Tobi Katō disposed of Murasame by the very unmagical trick of feeding it poisoned fried rice, whereupon the dog died instantly. He then scaled the walls, jumped over the moat (*tobi* can be translated as either 'flying' or 'jumping') and at the dead of night evaded the guards completely to reach the room where the *naginata* lay. To demonstrate the extent of his skills Tobi Katō not only took the *naginata*, but carried off on his back an 11-year-old servant girl.

Naturally, Kenshin was most impressed, and took Katō into his service. But others were jealous of him and plotted his downfall. Hearing that Naoe Kanetsugu was planning to kill him Katō fled, and sought employment with Kenshin's rival Takeda Shingen, where he began to serve one of Shingen's chief vassals. It proved an unwise move to make, because Shingen suspected that he was a double agent. He accused Katō of a theft, and had him quietly put to death.[13]

12 THE FLOATING WORLD

At about the same time that the author of *Okufuji Monogatari* was claiming that the ninja Nakagawa Shōshunjin could transform himself into a bird or an animal, the first printed illustration of a ninja – in fact, probably the first illustration of any sort of ninja – appeared in Japan.

Japan was now at peace. The Shimabara Rebellion had long been crushed, and the nation had cut itself off from all but minimal contact with the outside world. The samurai class ruled supreme, but the society they controlled was rapidly changing, and the first ninja picture was but one of a thousand different images of life in Japan during the early Edo Period that came to represent the popular culture of the *ukiyo*, or the 'floating world'. *Ukiyo* was originally a Buddhist expression signifying a release from this transient world of sorrows, but it came to mean much more than that, and became a positive seeking out of pleasure, which was the most attractive by-product of the peace which the iron rule of the Tokugawa brought to Japan. The samurai was now an urban dweller divorced from primary production, his needs being met by the farmers who toiled in the countryside and by the increasingly wealthy merchant class who shared his cities. It is this growing prosperity of the merchant class, coupled with a increasing degree of literacy at all levels in society, that provided the impetus for the *ukiyo*. In cities such as Edo were theatres, brothels, restaurants and teahouses, where intrigue, love affairs and excitement were to be found. To paraphrase the words of one commentator, the swaggering, sword-carrying samurai who formed the government restricted the rest of the population from doing anything with their lives except making love and making money, and the samurai were desperate to join in.

Popular literature provided a means whereby the idle, the timid or the curious could enjoy the *ukiyo* at secondhand. Until the Edo Period printing had been almost entirely restricted to the production of Buddhist texts. The *ukiyo* presented the printing industry with the opportunity of feeding a growing mass market for inexpensive books on secular themes, and many of these were well illustrated. There are not that many depicting ninja, but those that exist are sufficient to enable one to trace the development of the visual image of the ninja as a parallel to his transformation in popular thought from *shinobi* to superman.

One of the earliest subjects for mass production of printed books were editions of the military chronicles and *gunkimono*, which were regarded as edifying reading for the samurai class at a time when there was no certainty that the years of peace were going to last. One of these provides the example of the first ninja in art. He is the Hōjō's champion *rappa* Fuma (or Kazama) Kotarō, who appears in an illustration to a printed edition of the

The pleasure quarter of Yoshiwara

In this book illustration by Suzuki Harunobu, two gallants, one of whom is in firm control of his female companion, converse as they pass in the street of Yoshiwara. Note the headcowls, which are most like a ninja's on the tiny figure shown inside the gate. These figures are a convention in this genre, and are telling the moral of the story. (Courtesy of Christie's, London.)

Fuma Kotarō in action

This bold illustration of Fuma (or Kazama) Kotarō is probably the earliest printed depiction of anyone identified as a ninja. The demonic Kotarō watches as his band of rappa *cause havoc in the camp of the Takeda. (From a woodblock-printed edition of the* Hōjō Godai-ki *[1659]; private collection.)*

Hōjō Godaiki which was published in 1659. The pictures in these books are very interesting, representing as they do some of the earliest attempts at the art form of the illustrated book that was to blossom during the following century. The pictures are comparatively crude compared to what was to come later, but they are very effective. The depiction of Fuma Kotarō certainly conveys the air of 'superman' about him, and although it is not the conventional modern idea of the black-clad ninja, it certainly shows the demonic and mysterious nature of a ninja. His face looks very much like a demon's mask from the *Nō* theatre, with the high forehead reminiscent of the god Fukurokuju (as in Jōshin's description), his big eyes and nose, and his black whiskers. He is clearly shown as being much taller than his companions, which is brought out with most clarity in the second picture where he is standing beside them.

Elsewhere in the same book are two illustrations which refer to the story of the *shinobi* called *kusa*, who lay in wait for the Hōjō scouts. Once again there is no attempt made to dress them in black. They are instead conventionally dressed as the lower class *ashigaru*, having a mixture of weapons and armour, and only lightly protected legs.

This edition of the *Hōjō Godaiki* was in fact predated by a woodblock-printed illustrated edition of the *Heike Monogatari* dated 1656, which contains illustrations of the ninja incidents discussed earlier. Taira Tadamori is shown with the dummy dagger in his hand, and there is obvious consternation among his companions. In a later volume in the series we see a very good illustration of the two brothers Kawara Jirō and Kawara Tarō who temporarily abandoned their horses for a night raid. They are shown inside Ichi-no-tani's outer defence walls, and one has fallen dead from the arrows fired back by the Taira. In 1698 an illustrated edition of the *Taiheiki* was printed which shows brilliantly Kumawaka's escape from the house of Homma Saburō. Saburō is lying transfixed, with blood pouring from him, while Kumawaka uses the bamboo to drop over the moat.

Another century has to go by before we see the beginning of the image of the ninja in black. One of the earliest appears in the *Ehon Taikō-ki*, and is a superb picture of the ninja Kimura Hitachi-no-suke climbing in to Fushimi castle. The *Ehon Taikō-ki* is a romance by Takenouchi Kakusai based on the life of Hideyoshi, and illustrated by Okada Gyokuzan. It was published in Osaka in 1802, and banned by the Shogunate in 1804 because of the way it dealt with the Toyotomi, whom the Tokugawa had supplanted. The incident depicted is almost certainly fictional, but the detail, down to the hooked rope, is the best proof that exists that the image of the ninja as a man in black was immediately recognisable at the end of the eighteenth century. Here is the classic ninja attacking a castle, an image of noble daring and romance. Elsewhere in the book other ninja are shown raiding a house and taking a captive, but they are not dressed completely in black, and their leader appears to be wearing a fire helmet. A ninja similar to the one in the *Ehon Taikō-ki* appears in a much reproduced page (not shown here) in the *Manga* (*Random Sketches*) by Hokusai (1760–1849). Hokusai published the *Manga* as a series over a period of several years from 1814 onwards, and the ninja appears on a page along with several other martial arts subjects. He is climbing a rope, presumably to enter a castle.

Some of the best illustrations of ninja in books appear in the *Nise Murasaki Inaka Genji*, a parody of the *Tale of Genji* which became a popular novel of the later Edo Period and sold over 10,000 copies. The original *Genji Monogatari* was written in the tenth century, and its imitation was written by Ryūtei Tanehiko (1783–1843) and published in

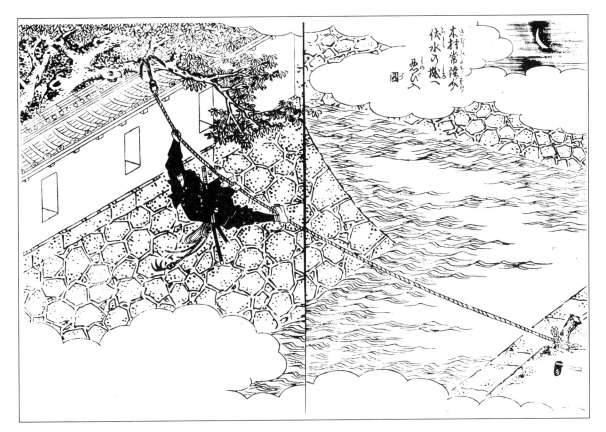

Attacking a castle
This very important book illustration is one of the earliest datable printed illustrations of a ninja dressed in the traditional black costume, and although both the character and the incident may well be fictional it provides firm proof that the image of the black-clad ninja is not a modern phenomenon but was well-established by the beginning of the nineteenth century. The caption reads, 'Kimura Hitachi-no-suke enters Fushimi Castle in secret'. Note the detailed reproduction of use of the climbing device, down to the mallet for driving in the stake. (From Ehon Taikō-ki, *a romance based on the life of Toyotomi Hideyoshi by Takenouchi Kakusai, and illustrated by Okada Gyokuzan, published in Ōsaka by Kobayashi Rokubei in Kyōwa 2 [1802].)*

Edo between 1828 and 1842 with illustrations by Kunisada (1786–1865). Its success was the result of the ability of Tanehiko, who was an intellectual of samurai stock and had a profound knowledge of classical literature. In his version he presented a 'Genji for the times'. Its hero is Prince Mitsuuji, son of the *shōgun* Ashikaga Yoshimasa. Masquerading as a libertine and dandy he fights against the plots of certain wicked subjects who are trying to choose a suitable heir with whom to destabilise and control the *shōgun*'s family. There are three pages of ninja. In one the hero of the work tackles a ninja who has made his way into the ladies' quarters, and pins him to the ground using a hold of *jūjutsu* while he takes the assailant's sword triumphantly in his other hand. In a further section (not included here) three men, two of whom, according to the text, 'had the appearance of *shinobi*', attack another in the street. But the best is that of an attack by a ninja on the Prince himself, who appears to be the aesthete lost in the rapture of his *koto*-playing and the brilliance of the moon, oblivious to the fact that a ninja is behind him with a drawn

An attack on Prince Mitsuuji

A ninja, dressed fully in black, draws his sword in readiness to strike down his victim, who is apparently lost in his contemplation of the moon and his playing of the koto. (From Nise Murasaki Inaka Genji, *a parody on the* Tale of Genji *by Ryūtei Tanehiko and illustrated by Utagawa Kunisada, published in Edo between 1828 and 1842; this version is from the 1927 reprint in the series* Nihon Meicho Zenshū.)

sword. This latter ninja is almost the perfect modern image. He is all in black except for his sword belt, and wears the open work sleeves that are often seen in modern pictures. But Mitsuuji is aware of his presence, and as the master swordsman he takes full control of the situation, even though he has his back to the ninja:

... without a word the mysterious person whose face was covered drew his sword. Mitsuuji, without a moment's delay, reached out his left hand, while with his right he continued to play the *koto*. The intruder, irritated by his behaviour, drew his sword again. ...[1]

The *Ehon Toyotomi Kunki* (which is sometimes written in the older style of *Yehon Toyotomi Kunki*), is a later work on the same theme as the *Ehon Taikō-ki*, the life of Hideyoshi, published between 1857 and 1884. This was illustrated by the greatest master of the warrior print, Kuniyoshi (1798–1861). Only one page shows ninja. It is of an incident sometime subsequent to the murder of Oda Nobunaga in 1582. The ninja are followers of Hideyoshi's general Fukishima Masanori, and are acting as spies to discover

126

Prince Mitsuuji overpowers a ninja
The hero of Nise Murasaki Inaka Genji *delights the terrified ladies by disarming a ninja. (From* Nise Murasaki Inaka
Genji, *a parody on the* Tale of Genji *by Ryūtei Tanehiko and illustrated by Utagawa Kunisada, published in Edo betwen
1828 and 1842; this version is from the 1927 reprint in the series* Nihon Meicho Zenshū.)

what plotting is going on between Shibata Katsuie, Takigawa Kazumasu and Oda Nobutaka, the conspiracy that eventually led to the Battle of Shizugatake. They both wear a
black sleeveless jacket and head cowl over their ordinary clothes.

   The story of the loyal *Forty-seven Rōnin* entered popular literature and the theatre as a
fictionalised play. The night attack made by the *rōnin* to carry out their act of vengeance
on Kira Yoshimoto implies secrecy and darkness, and one or two book illustrators have
chosen to depict the *rōnin* in dress indistinguishable from ninja. Sadahide (1807–73)
illustrated a book on the *Chūshingura*, (one version of the fictional story), in which he
chooses to depict certain members of the loyal 47 in almost complete ninja garb when
they are carrying out their raid on Kira's mansion. Two in particular are very fine, with
large black headcowls. Another print by Kunisada II (1823–80) (Plate 20), which is
actually an illustration to the *kabuki* play *Kanadehon Chūshingura*, shows two perfect
ninja, holding a woman captive and shining a dark lantern (which bore a candle on a
swivel, and had highly polished inner sides) into her face.

Ninja spies by Kuniyoshi
Spies sent by Fukshima Masanori listen to a secret conference betwen Shibata Kaysuie, Takigawa Kazumasu and Oda Nobutaka, who are planning to dislodge Hideyoshi from the position of pre-eminence he has acquired following Oda Nobunaga's death. (From Yehon Toyotomi Kunki, *a romance on the life of Hideyoshi by Ryūsuitei Tanekiyo, illustrated by Kuniyoshi, published between 1857 and 1884; private collection.)*

The Forty-seven Rōnin as ninja (I)
This illustration is from a Chūshingura, *the fictionalised version of the story of the* Forty-seven Rōnin, *illustrated by Sadahide. The character is wearing full ninja garb above waist level. (Private collection.)*

青物屋甚兵衛の話

Kabuki

The other great artistic element of the *ukiyo* is the woodblock colour-print or *ukiyo-e*, where the colour and excitement of the *demi-monde* of Edo are depicted vividly. Because of severe government censorship during the Tokugawa Period printmakers found it virtually impossible to depict historical figures in any way connected with the Tokugawa family. There were ways round it, such as the depiction of actors playing rôles based on historical personages, or of heroes designed to uplift morality by their example. There were further restrictions on the production of prints in the austerity measures of 1842, which were designed to improve morality and reduce extravagance, so laws banned the depiction of *kabuki* actors, courtesans and *geisha*. Instead designs had to be based on figures of loyalty and filial piety. As a result the printmakers started producing sets of actors in roles of loyal heroes from the past, or of ladies that were paragons of virtue. For these reasons there are virtually no prints of ninja assassinations, and we have to wait until the Meiji Period for the superb print which appears on the front cover and was drawn by the late master Toyonobu and published in 1883.

The prints that found their way through the government regulations were widely used as advertising material for the plays and the theatres, and also as souvenirs for a popular actor. Such prints were produced in their thousands, and readily obtainable for the same price, Tinios reminds us, as a haircut or a bowl of noodles.[2] They were sold to a public that loved to see pictures of their favourite actors (all parts were played by men from quite early on), who were followed with the fervour given to modern movie stars. As I noted in *Samurai Warlords*, the *kabuki* plays were the soap-operas of their day, the plots drawn from actual instances of family feuds within the upper classes and exaggerated out of all proportion, or heart-rending melodramas of everyday life. The strict government supervision noted above tried to control the theatres along with their prints, and made sure that they upheld morality and did not make any comment on contemporary politics, hence the changing of names and places of classic contemporary stories such as the *Forty-seven Rōnin*. During the first century of its existence the government even made several ineffective attempts to ban *kabuki*, and members of the samurai class were forbidden to attend. All was to no avail and, the more the flamboyant and boisterous *kabuki* was restricted, the more popular it became. The prints from the *kabuki* theatre reflected all this in their ephemeral nature.

Most of the woodblock prints of ninja which have survived therefore relate directly to certain plays of the *kabuki* theatre in which ninja play a part, and the play *Meiboku Sendai Hagi*, written originally for the puppet theatre in 1777, manages to give us the best known portrayal of a ninja, or at any rate a magician, in the theatre. The plot is based on the true story of a succession dispute within the Date family of Sendai in northern Japan, whereby a senior retainer of the family was plotting to take control of the infant heir. In the play all the names are changed, as is the plot, and other characters are introduced, including the ninja Nikki Danjō, nephew of the main plotter Oe Onitsura, who stands to inherit the family wealth should the young heir be disposed of.[3]

The Forty-seven Rōnin as ninja (II)
Another page from Sadahide's Chūshingura, *showing one of the gallant forty-seven climbing a ladder. (Private collection.)*

130

流石に時のふるとやなり伯と袴起一路中を登固もなくん細めの高呼が俯ふるきが塀に揚のうしろを見て佐藤登っとそ伯がてと把を扶け登らーながり夫より▲

The third and fourth acts of the play contain the ninja element. Masaoka, the nurse to the young heir Tsurukiyo, is afraid lest any food brought to him may have been poisoned by the conspirators, and she has trained her own infant son Senmatsu to taste all the food offered to his young lord, a noble and sacrificial samurai duty performed by this young child.

Two ladies in the pay of the villain bring some cakes, which Senmatsu dutifully takes, then suddenly kicks the box over, warning his playmate that they are poisoned. Realising that her plot is about to be discovered, the first conspirator, Yashio Gozen, pretends to be angry with Senmatsu for helping himself to the *shōgun*'s gift that was meant for Tsurukiyo, and in her mock fury takes a knife and cuts little Senmatsu's throat. His mother Masaoka sits as if turned to stone, and Yashio Gozen exits, leaving behind her companion Sakae Gozen, who watches Masaoka intently from behind her fan. Surely, she thinks, this woman Masaoka must be in on the plot, for no normal mother could restrain her grief when her own child is killed?

So convinced is Sakae Gozen that Masaoka is one of the gang that she praises Masaoka for her cunning, and gives her a list of the other conspirators.

Once Sakae Gozen has left, Masaoka can afford to let herself grieve and, while she is weeping over her dead son, who has died so honourably in the service of his lord, Yashio Gozen returns and tries to kill her. Masaoka fights back, and kills Yashio instead, but as they struggle the scroll of the conspirators falls out of her sleeve. Suddenly, a large grey rat appears running about the stage. It grabs the scroll in its mouth and runs off with it. The rat is none other than the nephew Nikki Danjō, who is adept at the magic arts, and by the practice of *ninjutsu* has learned how to transform himself into a rat.

Act Four opens with the loyal retainer Arajishi Otokonosuke on guard on the floor below the heir's room. He sees the rat scuttling past, and tries to stamp on it, then aims a series of blows at it with his iron fan. (See Plate 7, which is a print of this incident by Kunishū.) He wounds the rat on the head, but it wriggles away and escapes down one of the *hanamichi*, the platforms to the front of the *kabuki* stage. There is a sudden cloud of smoke, and the rat vanishes. The print by Kunisada shows the marvellous use of a trapdoor half way down the *hanamichi* by which means the rat is transformed back into Nikki Danjō. He rises from the floor like the demon king, with the scroll still clamped between his teeth, performing a *mudrā* with his fingers as he does so. Note how ropes and pulleys haul the trapdoor platform to the *hanamichi* surface, lit by candles carried on poles. The stagehands in their black garb look remarkably like ninja, but this is merely a convention of the *kabuki* theatre that signifies nothingness.

This pose of Nikki Danjō is one of the famous *mie* of the *kabuki* theatre, whereby at a crucial moment the action freezes into a rigid pose, described once very aptly as a 'visual exclamation mark'. Such *mie*, which are difficult to perform well with the actor's face and limbs contorted, were always cues for applause from the audience, and formed the subject of many of the prints produced about *kabuki*. Prints of Nikki Danjō's *mie* are

Nikki Danjō rises from beneath the stage
Nikki Danjō is the most famous ninja in the theatrical repertoire. He rises through a trap door, his sudden appearance on the stage marking his transformation back into human form from that of a rat, hence the fact that the scroll, which contains a list of his fellow conspirators, is clenched between his teeth. (From a print by Kunisada, 1860; private collection.)

commonly reproduced in books about ninja with no explanation of the context, so it may be thought that to hold a scroll in one's mouth was part of ninja magic, while in reality the scroll is there simply because Nikki Danjō has up to that point been a rat! In the second print of Danjō which I have chosen for this book the scroll of the conspirators has fallen open to reveal the list of names, but in the print the names are actually those of actors. At the end of the play Nikki Danjō, in full human form, attempts to stab the loyal retainer, Geki, but is himself overcome and killed.

It is doubtful whether the character of Nikki Danjō can be regarded as a ninja in terms of the definition we have adopted for this book, but his magic powers, attributed to *ninjutsu*, are stated very clearly. Another *kabuki* character with magic powers is Tenjiku Tokubei, the daring sailor who reached India whom I discussed in Chapter 11. He appears in the *kabuki* play *Kikutsuki Irifune Banashi*. He is supposed to be an expert at *ninjutsu*, and specialises in toad magic. The print shown in the colour plates is of Tokubei making the magical *mudrā* with his fingers, about to turn himself into a giant toad. The toad is beginning to emerge from behind him. The print is by Kunihiro and is of 1820.

The other prints depict two minor plays of the *kabuki* repertoire which show actors dressed in a similar fashion to ninja, or have some other connection. The first, by Toyokuni and of 1804, shows the famous actor Bando Mitsugorō (1755–1831) as a myste-rious ninja-like figure with Iwai Kanshirō as a female pilgrim. It is a scene from a play called *Kikuzumō Mikurai Sadame*. The ninja is dressed with the black clothing known as *suami*. The other is a four-person *mie* from *Yukimochidake Furisode Genji*, as drawn by Kiyonaga. It was first performed in 1785, and is an example of a *danmari*, or 'pantomime'. The actors are supposed to be fighting in the dark, and freeze in a *mie* of great power. The central character is an *abura bozū*, or 'oil priest'. His hair is dishevelled, indicating his dissipated nature. The figure in the foreground is most like a ninja, with black leggings and sleeves, and thunder and lightning occur as he draws his sword.

We noted earlier the print from *Kanadehon Chūshingura* by Kunisada II. This artist was a pupil of Kunisada, who also did a series of prints of scenes from the same play. In one (not shown here) there is a *shinobi* who is identified as such in the caption. He is sneaking up behind Ōboshi Yuranosuke, who is the character in the play who corres-ponds to the historical Ōishi Kuranosuke, leader of the avenging *rōnin*. The *shinobi* is not, however, dressed in black. A black-clad figure, however, appears in one of Kunisada's other theatre prints being overcome by a guard. The action takes place in front of a lady, so the figure could be a ninja who has broken in, but he has no head covering. Apart from this detail the image is perfect.

The Meiji Restoration removed many of the restrictions of the Tokugawa, allowing the woodblock print a final flourish before it was overtaken by modern technology. It is this we have to thank for the superb print by Toyonobu (who died in 1886), which appears in Plate 15. Its subject matter, the attempt on Nobunaga's life by Manabe Rokurō,

Bando Mitsugorō as a ninja?
This print by Toyokuni 1 (1810) shows the actor Bando Mitsugorō in a scene from the play Kikuzumō Mikurai Sadame. *Whilst he is dressed all in black, it is unlikely this character represents a ninja. (Private collection.)*

134

坂東三津五郎

岩井半四郎

豊国画

135

has been discussed in Chapter 5, but it shows us clearly that by 1883 the ninja's image was well established as a man in black.

Erotic Art

The prints so far discussed, particularly the Toyonobu, show the ninja in a very romantic light, as a clever magician, or as the brave warrior climbing into a castle at dead of night. But there is another side to the ninja image which is one of violence and menace, and it is not one that must be ignored if we are to appreciate the whole picture.

One little known use of the ninja in art is as a subject for eroticism. With no tradition of the nude, which could be seen in the flesh everywhere, Japanese erotic art concentrated almost exclusively on the sexual act, showing every conceivable combination of posture and situation, with much use of elaborate detail. Several series of prints and book illustrations show rape or other sexual violence towards women, and the image of the ninja as a mysterious and evil figure who breaks into a house by night has provided the basis for a number of illustrations depicting the ninja as a rapist. It is, however, curious, and not a little embarrassing to note that these explicit pictures actually provide some of the best illustrations of ninja at any time. A somewhat crude book illustration attributed to Tsukioka Sahei of a ninja seducing a servant girl may be one of the earliest depictions of the ninja as a man in black. He appears to be wearing a black costume with a head cowl, but as he is also wearing a helmet on his head, which is similar in shape to the helmets worn when supervising the control of fires, he may just be an ordinary samurai who had adopted the firecloak and helmet as a means of concealing his identity. An amusing erotic touch is provided by the presence of another couple making love on the opposite page, eyeing the 'ninja' and his companion with some interest.[4]

The imagery is clearer in the illustration by Utamaro (1750–1806) for the book *Ehon Takara-gura*, which appears in Plate 12. The ninja has broken into a mansion. He has a sword, and a saw in his belt, and is dressed entirely in black. He has slid the *shōji* to one side and his dark lantern reveals in its beam of light a couple making love. Here the ninja is a mere spectator, leaving to the viewer's imagination what he intends to do to the lovers. Like the illustration described in the preceding paragraph, this scene could also be considered titillating, and has a certain humour about it.

There exists however another book illustration, in the *Ehon Futami-gata*, probably by Hokusai (though it may be by Utamaro), which leaves nothing to the imagination. The detail of the ninja's costume is perfect, and it may well be one of the earliest pictures of a ninja as a man in black, pre-dating even the *Ehon Taikō-ki* castle attack. It is a picture of a ninja raping a woman, and it delivers a totally different message from Utamaro's Peeping Tom. This ninja's victim is bound by the arms and has apparently been beaten unconscious. As the ninja rapes her, he makes a threatening gesture with his sword to where the woman's husband, helpless to assist her, is also tied up and has been forced to watch. The subtlety of the other scene has been replaced by a casual relish at the cruelty and

Mie with a ninja
A print by Kiyonaga (about 1790) from the play Yukimochidake Furisode Genji. *The scene is a four-person* mie, *and has great presence. Thunder and lightning occur as the ninja character draws his sword. (Private collection.)*

violence involved, and serves as a timely reminder to us that whatever thrilling gloss we may place on the ninja nowadays, his activities were always both undercover and underhand. There is also a very similar rape scene a century later by Eisen (1864–1905) where the woman is tied up but struggling valiantly and kicking out at the man. The assailant is dressed much like a ninja but has a white head cowl.[5]

Yoshitoshi (1839–92) who was a pupil of Kuniyoshi and probably the last great master of *ukiyo-e*, never shrank from the full depiction of rape, murder or mutilation, often with much blood in evidence, but he does not seem to have used a ninja as protagonist in any of his prints. However the image, if not the figure, of a ninja appears very dramatically in one print of his series *Eimei Nijūhachi shūku* of 1866. This is an illustration to a poem based on the *kabuki* play *Otokodate Gosho no Gorozō*. The story is briefly as follows. Gosho no Gorozō is an *otokodate*, a 'chivalrous fellow' of the townsman class, who defends with his sword his life and his rights against his samurai betters. He is married to Tsuji, a former servant girl in the same household, and they have both been banished because of their love. Poverty has forced Tsuji to become a courtesan, and it is considered etiquette for a courtesan who is married to entertain only guests of her own choosing, not a certain Hoshikage Doemon, whose advances she repulsed many years before, but who has now returned to plague her again. Gorozō's former master has by now fallen on hard times, and Gorozō, in spite of his banishment, is determined to help him out by getting money for him. His wife takes his part, and when she is offered a large sum of money for her favours by Doemon she reluctantly accepts, meaning to help her husband's cause. But then, because of the disgrace this will bring her, she intends to commit suicide afterwards. Unfortunately, Gorozō is angry at her apparent faithlessness, and refuses to accept the money. Poor Tsuji has now to set off to complete her side of the bargain, but her friend and colleague O-shu bravely offers to go in her place. O-shu realises what Gorozō will probably do to his wife and her client, and she is quickly proved right. Gorozō is lying in wait for them, and kills O-shu, thinking in the poor light that it is his wife. He then realises his mistake and engages Doemon in a fierce swordfight. He kills Doemon and then himself. Such is the stuff of high tragedy in the *kabuki* theatre.[6]

When faced with the challenge of representing such devotion and slaughter in one print Yoshitoshi has chosen to use some remarkable symbolism. He shows the jealous and doomed Gorozō (with O-shu's head tied to his waist?), standing with a blood-stained sword. The cherry blossoms fall around 'blown by the wind from distant Fuji' according to the caption on the print, thus representing the short and tragic lives of the girls of the *ukiyo*. But how to represent the force of evil that lurks behind Doemon's desire for the woman? What image can Yoshitoshi adopt that will sum up for thousands of print buyers the remorseless adversary, the cruel inevitability of fate, while preserving the reality of the swordsman Doemon appearing out of the night? He chooses to give us a colossal ghostly ninja with no eyes and a huge sword. The figure is both mysterious and very menacing, and together with Hokusai's coldly calculating rapist epitomises the factors of ruthlessness and evil that cannot, and should not, ever be divorced from the otherwise romantic and sanitised image of the ninja which we cherish today.

A Ninja seducer

This book illustration by Tsukioka Sahei (ca 1770) shows an intruder dressed like a ninja seducing a servant girl. He is wearing what appears to be a fire helmet. Her comments on the experience appear above her head. This may be one of the earliest depictions of a ninja-like figure in black. (Private collection.)

The modern ninja boom
Two examples, one from Japan and one from Yugoslavia, showing how popular the ninja have become all round the world, spawning comics, films and books.

Hatsumi in action
Dr Masaaki Hatsumi must take most of the credit for rediscovering Japan's ninja past and making it known, both in Japan and in the West. This photograph was taken at the 1988 course conducted by Dr Hatsumi in Wimbledon, London. He is demonstrating an attack against two opponents. (Author's collection.)

13 NINJA TODAY

We approach the final chapter with two contradictory images of the ninja in mind. On the one hand we have the ruthless, mysterious and deadly silent assassin who, in his refusal to face the enemy head on, is the antithesis of the samurai ideal. On the other we have a romantic figure, ahead of his time in military technology, skilled in weaponry and the martial arts, who thereby represents the epitome of the samurai qualities. This is a strange paradox, and one that is reflected in modern manifestations of the ninja in the twentieth century.

A Modern Ninja?

If there is a modern army equivalent of the ninja, one candidate would be the intelligence officer. So is there any evidence of *ninjutsu* in the intelligence-gathering operations of the Japanese army? On the face of it there is very little. According to an article by Ian Nish, Japan used intelligence officers from very early on in the Meiji Period, and sent them to mainland Asia, especially China, from 1884 onwards. A British observer, writing in 1903, spoke of Japanese officers watching the Russians:

. . . the numerous itinerant Japanese who patrol Manchuria from end to end in various guises, gathering information of the minutest nature. In the event of a war with Russia, Japan will find herself in possession of detailed information. . . .[1]

The subject of Nish's paper, Ishimitsu Makiyo, was one of a number of intelligence officers who seem to have blended skilfully into the Chinese countryside before 1904. Things were very different 30 years later, as Nish notes in a paper about Captain Nakamura Shintarō, an intelligence officer operating in Manchuria in 1931, who was a far cry from one who practised the arts of invisibility:

. . . I was shown a photograph of Nakamura as he was about to set off on an expedition. In it he was dressed in a half-length coat, jodhpurs, riding boots and a fur hat with ear flaps. He looked just like an army officer, having a clipped moustache and a 'short back and sides' haircut. He bore little resemblance to a Chinese and obviously was not trying to look like one.[2]

To find anyone resembling a ninja either in appearance or training we have to turn to one of the most fascinating books to have come out of World War 2, the autobiography of Hirō Onoda, translated into English as *No Surrender – My Thirty-year War*. Second-Lieutenant Onoda emerged from the jungle of Lubang island in the spring of 1974, after 30 years of continuing World War 2 single-handed, convinced that the fighting was still going on and that Japan would be victorious. Onoda's extraordinary story is the best modern illustration of how the arts of the covert warrior turn conventional views of warfare upside down.[3]

Onoda was a graduate of the Nakano School, the Japanese Intelligence Training establishment in Tōkyō founded in 1938. In an article on the Nakano School Louis Allen discusses the Japanese concepts that lay at the heart of the students' training, which were *makoto* (integrity – more commonly translated as sincerity, a concept found throughout the history of the samurai) and *seishin* (spirit). By *seishin* was meant a fervent patriotism akin to the fervour of the anti-foreign samurai of the late Tokugawa Period, whose watchwords were *sonnō jōi* ('Revere the Emperor and expel the barbarian'). The first student supervisor at the school was Major Itō Samata to whom, according to Allen, this *seishin* mattered far more than either technique or common sense. In 1939, long before Britain and Japan were at war, he proposed a raid on the British Consulate in Kobe:

His projected attempt on the British consulate in Kobe was an example of *ninjutsu*, the art of invisibility. It represented the 'cowboy' stage of Nakano.[4]

Itō was convinced that the Consulate held documentary proof that the British had been offering bribes to certain Japanese politicians, and recruited two of his students to break in with him. Fortunately for all, the plan was leaked. Itō was court-martialled, and the students were sent overseas. From this time onwards the training became more realistic, and a branch of the Nakano School was set up at Futamata in 1944 for training men in guerrilla warfare. One tutor, at least, seems to have read his *Sonshi*.

His experience in counter-espionage with the Kwantung Army had taught him that it was not enough to arrest army agents. They had to be turned, otherwise their value was small. If you took a captured agent out of gaol, fed him with false intelligence (*nise jōhō*) and released him so that he returned to his control, he would be accepted as having carried out his exploit because he took some intelligence back with him.[5]

Some, like Onoda, were trained as agents who would stay behind on Pacific islands when the enemy invaded and keep on fighting. They were also deployed in several places throughout Japan in preparation for the expected invasion, and some were in position when the surrender broadcast came. All documents connected with the School were then burned, and the organisation dissolved.

As a consequence, we know the best details of its activities through its most famous, and undoubtedly most spectacularly successful graduate, who writes about his training as follows:

. . . the training was very different from what we had experienced at the officers' training school. There we were taught not to think but to lead our troops into battle, resolved to die if necessary. The sole aim was to attack enemy troops and slaughter as many as possible before being slaughtered. At Futamata, however, we learned that the aim was to stay alive and continue to fight as guerrillas as long as possible, even if this entailed conduct normally considered to be disgraceful.[6]

Later in the same chapter Onoda expands on this theme, which has strange echoes of Sun Tzu:

. . . we were taught that it was permissible to be taken prisoner. By becoming prisoners we were told we would place ourselves in a position to give the enemy false information. Indeed there might be times when we ought deliberately to let ourselves be captured. . . . Only insiders would ever know we had been engaged in secret warfare, and we would have to face the taunts of outsiders as best we could. Practically no one would be aware of our service to our country, but that is the fate of those engaged in secret warfare.[7]

He continues with an exposition of the philosophy that lay behind their conduct, which expands on Allen's note above:

In what then, can those engaged in this kind of warfare place their hope? The Nakano Military School answered this question with a simple sentence: 'In secret warfare, there is integrity'.

And this is right, for integrity is the greatest necessity when a man must deceive not only his enemies but his friends. With integrity – and I include in this sincerity, loyalty, devotion to duty and a sense of morality – one can withstand all hardships and ultimately turn hardship into victory.[8]

Onoda was posted to the Philippines, where he was ordered to lead the men stationed there as guerrillas in operations against the invading American forces. It was at this stage that he received the orders that were to change his life, and like the reference above to not being taken prisoner, epitomised the reversal of traditional values implied in the rôle of undercover soldier:

Then, with his eyes directly on me, he said, 'You are absolutely forbidden to die by your own hand. It may take three years, it may take five, but whatever happens we'll come back for you. Until then as long as you have one soldier, you are to continue to lead him. You may have to live on coconuts. If that is the case, live on coconuts! Under no circumstances are you to give up your life voluntarily'.[9]

Onoda was in fact to fight on long after he had but one soldier to lead, as his last companion died in 1972, two years before he finished his exile.

The full story of Onoda's single-handed resistance goes beyond the scope of this book, and is well worth reading in its entirety as an example of how the human mind can create a world for itself and then proceed to live in it. Every external stimulus was interpreted in the light of what Onoda and his companions believed to be true, even messages from home. Some examples have their amusing side, and are reminiscent of the story I quoted earlier about the ninja who hides in a tree and refuses to believe it is his comrade's voice calling to him. Photographs were dropped to the fugitives, on one of which were the family of Onoda's comrade Kozuka standing in front of their house.

Kozuka said, 'How do they expect me to believe this? Why would my family be standing in front of a new house that doesn't belong to us?' We did not know that Japanese cities had been extensively bombed and the city of Tokyo largely reduced to ashes.[10]

On one occasion, he received by parachute copies of magazines showing the prosperous Tōkyō streets full of cars, which led him to conclude that if Tōkyō looked like this then the war must be going Japan's way! He kept this up for 30 years, and was finally persuaded to give himself up only when his former commanding officer, who had since retired, was taken to Lubang and gave Onoda his orders.

The Ninja Boom
Onoda returned as a hero and a media personality, and to a new Japan where ninja and their ways had long since become a money-spinner. One of the earliest manifestations of this was a comic book series called *Ninja Bugeichō*, drawn by Sampei Shirato and published between 1959 and 1962. It was concerned with the fictional adventures of a ninja called Kagemaru, who falls foul of Oda Nobunaga. In one unforgettable frame Kagemaru's head is brought before Nobunaga, and introduces itself!

It was not long before the growing ninja craze in Japan spread overseas. In 1964 Ian Fleming published his novel *You Only Live Twice*, a James Bond story, and the first popular work in English to feature ninja. As such it undoubtedly had an influence. We meet the ninja first as Tanaka shows Bond a demonstration of their skills at his castle, which is used as their training ground:

... there came a whistle from above them on the ramparts and at once ten men broke cover from the forest to their left. They were dressed from head to foot in some black material, and only their eyes showed through slits in the black hoods. They ran down to the edge of the moat, donned oval battens of what must have been some light wood such as balsa, and skimmed across the water with a kind of skiing motion until they reached the bottom of the giant black wall. There they discarded their battens, took lengths of rope and a handful of small iron pitons out of pockets in their black robes and proceeded to almost run up the walls like fast black spiders.[11]

Later in his visit Bond is shown more examples from the ninja armament, which he learns that he is to use to carry out his mission:

... you will throttle him with the ninja chain you will be wearing round your waist . . . . The ninja clothing will give you complete protection. You will have a black suit for night. . .[12]

The above passage is quoted as an introduction to an interesting article prompted by *You Only Live Twice*, which appeared in *Newsweek* very soon after the book was published. Entitled '*Japan – a good cocktail*' it called the enthusiasm for ninja 'the latest craze to hit craze-prone Japan':

... today they enjoy a vogue which sweeps from toddlers to grandparents. Japanese cops are plagued by gangs of would-be ninja, and the Japanese press with discouraging regularity reports the misadventures of youngsters who seek to soar off rooftops or slip through drainpipes in approved ninja fashion. Sternly, Tokyo's daily Sankei Shimbun last week exhorted its readers: ' We warn against the ninja game . . . an abnormal hobby in which adults are also responsible.'[13]

The article was written two years before the death of Japan's last practising ninja, Fujita Seiko (1899–1966), which gave the anonymous journalist an opportunity for an interview:

... Seiko Fujita, a 65-year-old Tokyoite who styles himself the 'fourteenth master of the Koga school of ninjutsu.' Trained by his grandfather in the arts of the ninja, Fujita claims he can 'concentrate his senses' to see eight times better and hear fourteen times better than normal. To condition himself to pain, Fujita stuck hundreds of needles in his flesh and to learn to tolerate poison, he says, 'I ate sulphuric acid, rat poison, wall lizards, 879 glasses, 30 bricks.' (A glass was easy, he recalls thoughtfully, 'but it took me 40 minutes for a brick').

Fujita, who claims he is the last of the ninja and that the secrets of the craft 'will die with me' deplores the current commercialization of ninja in Japan'.[14]

The author goes on to mention that there were 200 ninja books then on sale in Japan, many of which involved sexual activities. A critic, he notes, described them as 'a good cocktail of nonsense, eroticism and cruelty', and added that 'eroticism and cruelty have always been the Japanese traditional favourites'. My discoveries of the book illustrations discussed in the previous chapter would appear to bear this out.

The article ends with the story of a 16-year-old boy who was caught in full ninja regalia of suit, mask, dagger, *shūriken* and all, inside the grounds of the old Imperial Palace in Kyōto. Why did he break in? Because, he explained, there was a heavy guard and he wanted to try out his technique.

The film of *You Only Live Twice* followed in 1967, and put ninja on the agenda of the English-speaking world in a way that no book could ever have done. Only a recent re-reading of the novel reminded me how widely the film's plot differed from that of the

144

The Iga festival
A ninja festival is held every year in Iga-Ueno. This is part of the parade by local people dressed as the city's most famous contribution to popular culture. (Author's collection.)

Interior of the Iga museum
Iga-Ueno is the centre for ninja enthusiasts in Japan. Beneath its reconstructed ninja house is this interesting museum containing models, weapons and armour associated with ninja. (Author's collection.)

Fleming original. The film's climax, and several incidents through the film, made exciting use of ninja, and set forever in the public's mind the image of a black-garbed assassin, superb at martial arts, and heedless of death. They were the perfect foil to a hero such as James Bond, who himself was renowned for physical skill and the ninja-like use of clever gadgets. Many memorable scenes were added to the book's original plot, such as the attempt on Bond's life by dripping poison down a thread, and the dramatic martial arts sequences at Himeji castle.

In 1966 and 1967, *Black Belt* magazine included a series on ninja by Andrew Adams with excellent photographs from film studios and several good shots of Hatsumi in action. The series was eventually published in book form in 1970, and remains a useful work, although the historical context presented is very wide of the mark. In 1969, Draeger's book on martial arts was published, with a good section on ninja, and its notorious recounting of the Kenshin murder story, to be followed by several books by Stephen Hayes, who went to Japan to learn *ninjutsu* from Dr Hatsumi.

I do not feel qualified to comment on the numerous techniques of *ninjutsu* which are now to be found being taught to aspiring 'modern ninja', but considering the remarks with which I concluded in Chapter 12 – where I drew attention to the fact that contemporary illustrations of ninja pull no punches over the unsavoury side of the activities of those whose trade was stealth and murder – it seems extraordinary to read claims by modern practitioners of *ninjutsu* that theirs is an ancient art of self-fulfilment. Yet these modern ninja, whatever the authenticity of their art, appear to have a sincere interest in Japan's martial past, unlike far too many of the practitioners of the 'serious' martial arts, who never seem capable of raising their noses from a single-minded quest to establish the purity of their style over that of all others.

There has of course been a considerable dilution of quality since ninja became so popular, and it is inevitable that many of the self-styled 'ninja masters' must be charlatans. I join with Hatsumi and Hayes in deploring this completely unregulated trend, which seems to promise little but injury and light wallets. When a 'course on *Ninjutsu*' can be advertised which offers 'ten per cent reduction to Registered Yamabushi', I tend to get a little sceptical!

The Ninja Heritage Industry

In the past decade, the ninja craze has taken off both in Japan and in the West, and there are several places in Japan where its tourist potential has been well realised. The centre of the popularisation in Japan is undoubtedly Iga-Ueno in Mie prefecture, which was not slow to realise the tourist potential in its own history. At the time of the Iga Revolt Ueno was the site of a temple called the Heiraku-ji, from which the men of Iga set out to meet the invader. Tsutsui Sadatsugu, heir of Tsutsui Junkei, built the first Ueno castle in 1585. Sadatsugu was deprived of his territory in 1608 on the grounds of bad management, and the castle passed to Tōdō Takatora (1556–1630), who had fought during Nobunaga's campaigns. At the instigation of Ieyasu, Takatora began work on a much larger edifice

The ninja village in Nagano
Iga and Koga do not have the monopoly of ninja tourist attractions in Japan. This is the map of the ninja village and 'theme park' near Nagano, which contains all sorts of exciting ninja activities for children, such as various climbing areas, and a shūriken firing range1

146

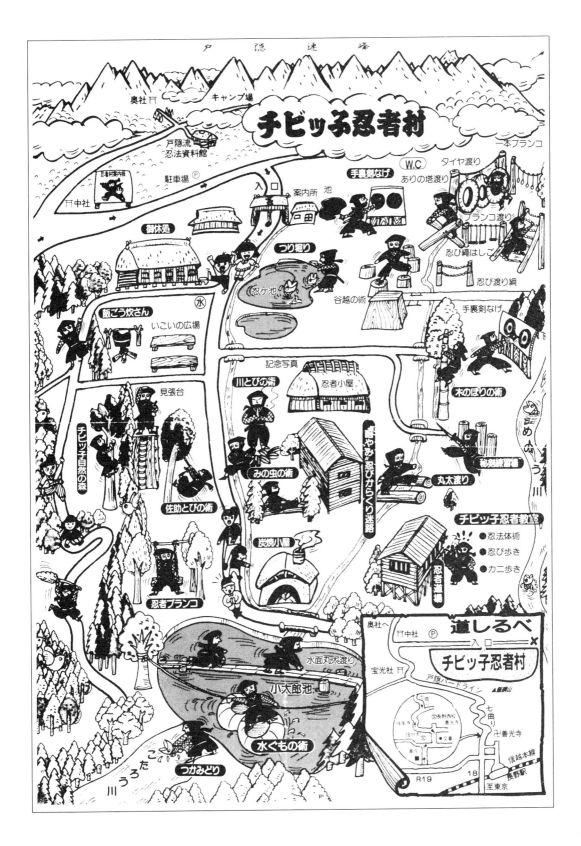

147

intended to be one of the three finest castles in Japan. Much use was made of the natural topography, and a moat was dug. Work was started on a five-storey keep, but a storm toppled it just before completion, and it remained without a keep until the Meiji Restoration. The present keep is a modern reconstruction.

The park in the castle grounds boasts a ninja house and a ninja museum. The house was moved to the park which surrounds the castle in 1964, and was originally the home of the ninja Takayama Tarōjirō. It contains several trap doors and concealed entrances, reminiscent of 'priest-holes' in England, which are demonstrated to the visitor by two fetching young lady ninja dressed in all-concealing ninja costumes, the effect of which is spoiled by the choice of bright pink or purple as a colour. The museum is built underneath the house and is very interesting. Among other things it has the archive of books, clothing and weaponry belonging to the 'last ninja' Fujita Seiko, and some good models of ninja in action. Ueno also stages an annual ninja festival, with a parade through the streets of gentlemen in suitable attire.

There is a smaller collection of ninja materials at the concrete Fushimi-Momoyama castle near Kyōto. Koga, the rival to Iga in its supply of *shinobi* mercenaries, now has a ninja theme park, including a 'firing range' for *shūriken*. There is also a theme park next to the battlefield of Sekigahara which has a replica of a *daimyō*'s mansion advertised as a 'ninja village'. One of its oddest reconstructions is the 'ferris-wheel' ladder I mentioned earlier for depositing an endless stream of ninja on to castle walls. A similar park, with much emphasis on activities for children, is to be found near Nagano. This one has an excellent collection of artefacts.

It is also significant of the hold ninja have on popular history that several genuinely old edifices now go to great pains to publicise some ninja connection for themselves. One is Nijō-jinya, a little house in Kyōto thrust into tourist prominence by a book called *Kyōto, a Contemplative Guide*.[15] Nijō-jinya was the home of Ogawa Hiraemon, a former samurai who had become a rice merchant, and the unique features which have enabled it to survive so long owe more to fire precautions than to anti-ninja devices, though it is by these that it is sold to visitors. It is a fascinating place to visit, and its defensive and fireproofing features, quite revolutionary at the time, include earthen doors and metal-sheathed roof sections. The flooring of the entrance hall has a built-in squeak like the nightingale floor of the better known Nijō castle. In the ceiling of the main reception room there is a square hole which appears to be solely to allow in light from the skylight window above it, but in fact the opening is directly above the place where a visitor would be sitting so that a guard could drop right on him should this be necessary. The guard chamber also allows whoever is in there to hear all conversation in the room below. Elsewhere in the house are removable floorboards disclosing ankle-breaking beams, and narrow hallways with low ceilings to discourage swordplay. Mosher reckons that none of the ninja features were ever used for the purpose for which they were intended, but the fireproofing certainly seems to have stood the test of time, and is the sole reason we can still enjoy it today.[16]

The ninja assassin – the perennial image
The popular image of the ninja as a black-clad, deadly assassin is effectively evoked in this page from the comic series Kozure Okami, *published in the U.S.A. as* Lone Wolf and Cub. *Note his use of the sword as an aid to scaling the wall.* (Lone Wolf and Cub © 1990, First Publishing Inc. and Global Communications Corp.)

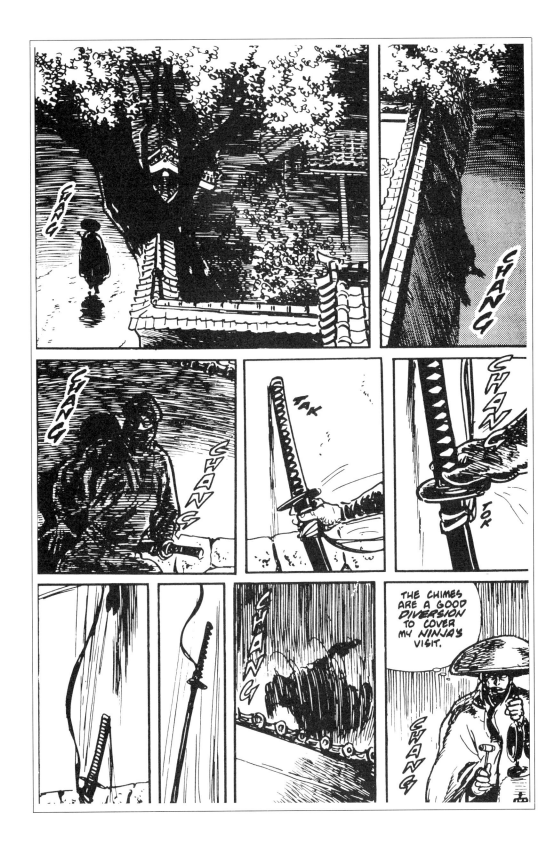

149

A further example is found in the Teramachi district of Kanazawa. Having escaped the bombing of the last war, Kanazawa has retained much of its past; and the Myōryū-ji has proved a jewel in the crown. The Myōryū-ji was one of a number of temples relocated to the outskirts of the city by the third *daimyō* Maeda Toshitsune (1593–1658), to provide an outer defence for Kanazawa. It possesses a number of secret rooms, concealed doors and secret passages, and is now inevitably known as *Ninja-dera*, but is not the less worth visiting for that. One of its most interesting features is the outer entrance door, which is approached up a short flight of stairs. The vertical surfaces of the stairs are only paper, as used on sliding screens, so that a guard could thrust a spear through to cut the legs of anyone trying to gain access. The sliding entrance door is in fact a double one, the inner of which slides across a hinged door which leads to a secret corridor, so that a person being pursued could give the impression of disappearing. There is also a completely hidden staircase to the third storey where there is a tea ceremony room. In the *tokonoma* is a rather ugly painting of Mount Fuji, which is hinged, and drops down to let a guard through. The temple's well is supposed to have a secret passage to the castle, which seems rather unlikely as the river is in the way.

So the ninja, it would appear, are definitely here to stay, but what is the secret of their popularity? First, the ninja cult takes the martial arts, enough of a cult in themselves, and transforms them into something superhuman. It adds the air of fantasy demanded now-adays by a post-Tolkien public fed on *Dungeons and Dragons* of which the most surprising example is the sudden popularity in the late 1980s/early 1990s of the *Teenage Mutant Ninja Turtles*. This remarkable phenomena, which began as a cartoonist's jest, has brought the world 'ninja' to a new generation. But what ninja they are! A gang of turtles, transformed in a sewer into superheroes, with skills at martial arts that James Bond's adversaries would have envied! No doubt, some ninja purists will scorn the Turtle cult, but these 'sub-humans' are no less fantastic than many of the 'super-humans' discussed earlier.

The ninja cult adds a touch of mystery to martial arts and offers the guarantee of supreme success – or death. Contrast this with Ivan Morris's *The Nobility of Failure* which appeared in 1975, at the time when the ninja craze in the West was getting under way. It is the classic study of the psychology of a very different archetype of the Japanese warrior, the man who devotes everything to his cause, accepts no compromise, and is finally beaten by his triumphant enemy, dying by his own hand secure in the conviction of his own unwavering sincerity. Yet this is not what the public want to hear; in the ninja they have the perfect answer for a ruthless world, whereby 'nobility of failure' is eclipsed by 'ignobility of success'. Nothing better illustrates the way in which the arts of the ninja turned traditional samurai values on their heads: the despised and feared ninja, whose calling was contradictory to everything the samurai stood for, have themselves become the 'super-samurai' of today.

NOTES AND REFERENCES

Chapter 1   The First Ninja

1   Miura Jōshin, *Hōjō Godai-ki* in *Sengoku Shiryō Sōshō* Series 2, Vol. 1, pp. 395–397.
2   Quoted in Sasama, *Buke Senjin Sahō Shūsei* p. 85.
3   Sun Tzu, *The Art of War*, translated by Samuel B. Griffith, p.145.
4   Sasama, *op.cit.* p. 84. *Buyō Benryaku* was compiled in 1684 by Kinoshita Gishun.
5   Sun Tzu, *op.cit.* p. 146.
6   Turnbull, *The Samurai – A Military History* p. 23.
7   Murdoch, *A History of Japan* Vol 1, pp. 630–631.
8   Machiavelli, *The Prince*, translated by George Bull, p.100.
9   There are several versions of the Yamato legend; see, for example, F. Hadland Davis, *Myths and Legends of Japan* pp. 51–52.
10 *ibid.* pp. 44–48; but see Keyes, *The Male Journey in Japanese Prints* pp. 50–53, for a different illustration and a very different interpretation.
11 Rabinovitch, *Shōmonki* pp. 92–95.
12 Sadler, *Heike Monogatari* Part 2, p. 17.
13 *ibid.* p. 145.
14 *ibid.* pp. 145–146.
15 *ibid.* p. 146.

Chapter 2   The Emperor's Ninja

1   Turnbull, *Samurai Warriors* pp. 29–30.
2   Yamada, *Ghenkō The Mongol Invasion of Japan* pp. 129–130.
3   McCullough, *The Taiheiki* p. 77.
4   *ibid.* p. 78.
5   *ibid.* p. 30.
6   *ibid.* p. 135.
7   *ibid.* p. 185.
8   Yamaguchi, *Ninja no seikatsu* p. 70.
9   Sasama, *Buke Senjin Sahō Shūsei* p. 83. I have been unable to find any definite date for the *Yoshōki*. The compiler was one Ichinin Kyoshi.

Chapter 3   Iga and Koga

1   Sansom, *A History of Japan 1334–1615* p. 287, is an example of a reference to pirates. For Ishikawa Goemon, see Watatani, *Bugei Ryūha Hyakusen* p. 19.

2   Sugiyama, *Nihon no Rckishi* 11 *Sengoku daimyō* p. 205.
3   *ibid.* p. 205.
4   Yūki, *Koga jōkaku gun* pp. 114–121.
5   Sugiyama, *op.cit.* p. 206.
6   Sugawara, *Lives of Master Swordsmen* p. 102
7   Turnbull, *The Lone Samurai and the Martial Arts* p. 77.
8   Turnbull, *Battles of the Samurai* p. 37.
9   Kurita, *Kaisei Mikawa Go-Fudo-ki* Vol. 1, p. 244.
10 Yamaguchi, *Ninja no seikatsu* p. 52.
11 *ibid.* p. 52.
12 Kurita, *op.cit.* p. 244.
13 *ibid.* p. 244.
14 Yamaguchi, *op.cit.* pp. 53–54.
15 Kurita, *op.cit.* p. 262.
16 The most accessible version of the *Bansen Shūkai* is in Imamura, *Nihon Budō Zenshū* Vol. 4, pp. 405–482. The Dodo story appears on p. 428.
17 Yamaguchi, *op.cit.* p. 208.
18 *ibid.* p. 208.

Chapter 4   The Loyal Ninja

1   Sasama, *Buke Senjin Sahō Shūsei* p. 83.
2   The *Chūgoku Chiran-ki* is reproduced in *Sengoku Shiryō Sōshō* 2nd series, Vol. 9, pp. 17–47. The *ninja* incident is on p. 21.
3   Yamaguchi, *Ninja no seikatsu* p. 75.
4   This appears to be a combination of two standard battle formations discussed in Sasama, *op.cit.* pp. 246–271. See also Turnbull, *Samurai Armies* pp. 11–12.
5. The *Hōjō Godai-ki* appears in *Sengoku Shiryō Sōshō* 2nd Series, Vol. 1. The *kusa* story is on pp. 395–397.
6   ibid. pp. 397–398.
7   *ibid.* p. 398.
8   *ibid.* pp. 398–400.
9   *ibid.* p. 400.
10 The *Ou Eikyō Gunki* appears in *Sengoku Shiryō Sōshō* 2nd Series, Vol. 3 and 4. The *ninja* story is in Vol. 4, p. 308.

Chapter 5   Assassins

1   Sadler, *Heike Monogatari* Part 1, p.3.

151

2   *ibid.* p. 6.
3   Sasama, *Buke Senjin Sahō Shūsei* p.82.
4   Yamaguchi, *Ninja no seikatsu* p. 70.
5   McCullough, *The Taiheiki* p. 47.
6   *ibid.* p. 48.
7   *ibid.* p. 48.
8   *ibid.* p. 49.
9   See Turnbull, *Samurai Warlords* p. 71, for an illustration.
10 Takahashi, *Hata sashimono* (passim). As this is a guide to Japanese heraldry, no information is given about the rôle the *bugyō* (commissioners) were expected to play, nor is there any source reference.
11 See the illustration, which is from the *Ehon Toyotomi-ki*; also Hayes, *The Mystic Arts of the Ninja* p. 5.
12 Adams, *Ninja – The Invisible Assassins* p. 160.
13 Momochi, *Kōsei Iran-ki* Vol. 4, p. 5.
14 Hatsumi, *Ninja ninpo gahō* p. 143.
15 Personal communication from James Shortt.
16 Sugiura, *Uesugi Kenshin no shi-in* p. 20.
17 The Uesugi Shrine at Yonezawa kindly supplied me with a photocopy of the relevant section of the chronicle, which is undated.
18 Watanabe, *Kenshin no nana fushigi* pp. 108–109. Watanabe also reminds us that the supposed 'diary' is not contemporary.
19 Personal communication. All comments of a medical nature are the results of a discussion the author had with a consultant pathologist regarding Kenshin's symptoms.
20 Anon., *Uesugi Kenshin-den*.
21 See Turnbull, *Samurai Warlords* and *Battles of the Samurai* for more detail on Kakizaki's early career.
22 Watanabe, *op.cit.* p. 108. The earlier part of this article discusses other evidence for the theory that Kenshin was a woman.
23 Quoted in Sugiura, *op.cit.* p. 19. Arai Hakuseki (1656–1725) was one of the most distinguished scholars of the early Edo Period.
24 *ibid.* p. 20.
25 Personal communication (as 19).
26 Letter to the author.
27 Letter to the author.

Chapter 6   The Iga Revolt

1   Saotome, *Ninja no sato ni shisu* p. 71. This is a useful article in that, although it is written as historical fiction, the author quotes from actual source materials.
2   Kōbe, *Seishū Heiran-ki* p. 589. The chronicle appears in the series *Kaitei shiseki shūran* Vol. 25, pp. 585–601. It was originally compiled in 1638.
3   *ibid.* p. 592
4   Momochi, *Kōsei Iran-ki* Vol. 2, p. 2. Momochi Orinosuke is the editor of the printed version of the anonymous chronicle, which was published in 1897.
5   *ibid.* p. 4
6   *ibid.* p. 4
7   *ibid.* p. 4.
8   *ibid.* p. 5.
9   *ibid.* p. 8.
10 *ibid.* p. 8.
11 *ibid.* p.11.
12 Ota, *Shinchōkō-ki* p. 262.
13 Momochi, *op.cit.* p. 12.
14 *ibid.* p. 12.
15 Kōbe, *op.cit.* p. 593.

Chapter 7   Destruction of Iga

1   Ota, *Shinchōkō-ki* p. 262.
2   Momochi, *Kōsei Iran-ki* Vol. 2, p. 13.
3   *ibid.* Vol. 3, p. 7.
4   *ibid.* p. 9
5   Kōbe, *Seishū Heiran-ki*, p.594.
6   Ota, *op.cit.* p. 332.
7   Momochi, *op.cit.* Vol. 3, p. 13.
8   *ibid.* p. 14.
9   *ibid.* p. 14.
10 *ibid.* Vol. 7, p. 4.
11 *ibid.* p. 5.
12 *ibid.* Vol. 4, p. 9.
13 *ibid.* Vol, 5, p. 11.
14 *ibid.* Vol. 6, p. 1.
15 *ibid.* p. 2.
16 *ibid.* p. 2.
17 *ibid.* p. 7.
18 *ibid.* p. 7.
19 Ota, *op.cit.* pp. 333–334.
20 *ibid.* p. 335.
21 *ibid.* p. 336.
22 Momochi, *op.cit.* Vol. 4, p. 5.

Chapter 8   Serving the Shōgun

1   Ota, *Shinchōkō-ki*, p. 334.
2   Kurita, *Kaisei Mikawa Go-Fudo-ki*, Vol. 2, p. 191.
3   *ibid.* pp. 191–192.
4   Sadler, *The Maker of Modern Japan*, p. 116.
5   Yamaguchi, *Ninja no seikatsu*, p. 21.
6   *ibid.* p. 91.
7   Oze, *Taikō-ki* Vol. 3, pp. 107–108.
8   Yamaguchi, *op.cit.* p. 261.
9   *ibid.* p. 262.
10 *ibid.* p. 265.
11 *ibid.* p. 267.
12 *ibid.* p. 267.
13 Turnbull, *The Samurai – A Military History* p. 255.
14 Ueno City, *Guide* (leaflet in English).
15 Yamaguchi, *op.cit.* p. 269.
16 *ibid.* p. 59.
17 Watatani, *Bugei ryūha hyakusen* p. 8.
18 Morris, *The Nobility of Failure* p. 164.
19 Yamaguchi, *op.cit.* p. 60.

20 *ibid.* p. 61.
21 *ibid.* p. 63.
22 *ibid.* p. 64.

Chapter 9   From Shinobi to Superman

1   Yamaguchi, *Ninja no seikatsu* p. 125.
2   Sugawara, *Lives of Master Swordsmen* p. 122.
3   Hatsumi, *Ninja ninpo gahō* p. 132.
4   Sugawara, *op.cit.* pp. 146–160 for a full account of his life.
5   Saotome, *Ninja no sato ni shisu* p. 71.
6   See photograph page 145.
7   Draeger, *Asian Fighting Arts* p. 130.
8   Watatani, *Bugei ryūha hyakusen* p. 124–125.
9   *ibid.* p. 125.
10 Yamaguchi, *op.cit.* p. 200.
11 *ibid.* p. 109.
12 *ibid.* p. 185.
13 Hatsumi, *op.cit.* p. 118, plus illustration.
14 Yamaguchi, *op.cit.* p. 205.
15 *ibid.* p. 196.

Chapter 10   Martial Arts

1   Yamaguchi, *Ninja no seikatsu* p. 139.
2   *ibid.* p. 140.
3   The most accessible version of the *Bansen Shūkai* is in Imamura, *Nihon Budō Zenshū* Vol. 4, pp. 405–482.
4   Yamaguchi, *op.cit.* pp. 244–247. There does not appear to be a modern version of the *Shōnin-ki*, which is in the National Diet Library, Tokyo.
5   Personal communication from Hatsumi.
6   Yamaguchi, *op.cit.* p. 223.
7   Sanford, *Shakuhachi Zen* pp. 411–440.
8   Yamaguchi, *op.cit.* p. 105, quotes this. See also Imamura, *op.cit.*
9   *ibid.* pp. 100–101.
10 Hatsumi, *Ninja ninpo gahō* p. 101 for an illustration.
11 I am indebted to Dr. Toshio Watanabe for this gem of information!
12 From the Kodansha encyclopaedia entry.
13 Sasama, *Buke Senjin Sahō Shūsei* p. 360.
14 From the Kodansha encyclopaedia entry.
15 Yamaguchi, *op.cit.* p. 104.
16 Kenkyūsha, *New Japanese English Dictionary* p. 1532.
17 Needham, *A History of Science and Civilisation in China* Vol. 5, Part 5, p. 311 contains the picture, which is also reproduced in Umezu, *Emakimono Sōshi.*
18 Yamaguchi, *op.cit.* pp. 169–170.
19 *ibid.* p. 98

20 All these devices, superbly drawn, are included in Hatsumi's *Ninja ninpo gahō* pp. 69–94.
21 Garbutt, *Military Works in Old Japan* p. 63.

Chapter 11   Magicians and Mystics

1   Adams, *Ninja – The Invisible Assassins* pp. 31–32, is merely a typical example. More recent works are better, such as Hayes, *The Mystic Arts of the Ninja*, which includes a series of useful pen portraits of famous ninja.
2   Swanson, *Shūgendō and the Yoshino-Kumano Pilgrimage* p. 56.
3   Blacker, *Initiation in the Shūgendō* p. 98.
4   Rotermund, *Die Yamabushi* p. 89.
5   De Visser, *The Tengu* p. 72.
6   Joly, *Legend in Japanese Art* pp. 364–365.
7   Watatani, *Bugei ryūha hyakusen* p. 124.
8   Murdoch, *A History of Japan* p. 584.
9   Joly, *op.cit.* p. 286.
10 *ibid.* p. 287.
11 Saunders, *Mudrā* p. 5.
12 McCullough, *The Taiheiki* p. 358.
13 Yamaguchi, *Ninja no seikatsu* p.202.

Chapter 12   The Floating World

1   Tanehiko, *Nise Murasaki Inaka Genji*, page as accompanying illustration.
2   Tinios, *Kunisada* p. 15.
3   Halford, S. & G., *The Kabuki Handbook* p. 212–220. See also Gunji, *Kabuki* p. 166.
4   Personal communication with H. Lühl.
5   *ibid.*
6   Halford, S. & G., *op.cit.* p. 300–303.

Chapter 13   Ninja Today

1   Nish, *Ishimitsu Makiyo* p. 1.
2   Nish, *Japanese Military Intelligence on the eve of the Manchurian Crisis* p. 23.
3   Onoda, *No Surrender – My Thirty-Year War.*
4   Allen, *The Nakano School* p. 11.
5   *ibid.* p. 12.
6   Onoda, *op.cit.* p. 32.
7   *ibid.* p. 33.
8   *ibid.* p. 34.
9   *ibid.* p. 44.
10 *ibid.* p. 125.
11 Fleming, *You Only Live Twice*, p. 95.
12 *ibid.* p. 114.
13 *Newsweek* 3 August 1964, p. 31.
14 *ibid.*
15 Mosher, *Kyoto – A Contemplative Guide* pp. 311–318.
16 *ibid.*

BIBLIOGRAPHY

Anonymous *Uesugi Kenshin-den* (Date unknown.)

Anonymous 'Japan – a good cocktail' *Newsweek* 3 August 1964.

Adams, Andrew 'A curriculum for assassins' *Black Belt* January 1967.

Adams, Andrew *Ninja – The Invisible Assassins* Los Angeles, 1973.

Addiss, Stephen *Japanese Ghosts and Demons* Kansas, 1983.

Allen, Louis 'The Nakano School' *Proceedings of the British Association for Japanese Studies* 1985.

Blacker, Carmen 'Initiation in the Shūgendō: the passage through the ten states of existence' in C.J. Blecker (ed.) *Initiation* 1965.

Bottomley, I. and Hopson, A. *Arms and Armour of the Samurai*, London, 1989.

Davis, F. Hadland *Myths and Legends of Japan*, London, 1913.

De Visser, M.W. 'The Tengu' *Transactions of the Asiatic Society of Japan* Vol. 36, Part 2, Yokohama, 1908.

Draeger, Donn and Smith, Robert *Asian Fighting Arts* Palo Alto, 1969.

Fleming, Ian *You Only Live Twice* London, 1964.

Fujibayashi, Masutake *Shōnin-ki* Ueno, 1681.

Fujibayashi, Yasutake *Bansen Shūkai* Ueno, 1676.

Garbutt, M. 'Military works in old Japan' *Transactions and Proceedings of the Japan Society* London, 1907.

Gunji, Masakatsu *Kabuki* Tokyo, 1985.

Halford, S. and G. *The Kabuki Handbook* Rutland, Vermont, 1956.

Hatsumi, Masaaki *Ninja ninpo gahō* Tokyo, 1977.

Hatsumi, Masaaki *Ima Ninja* Tokyo, 1981.

Hayes, Stephen *The Mystic Arts of the Ninja* Chicago, 1985.

Imamura, Yoshio *Nihon Budō Zenshū* Vol. 4, Tokyo, 1962.

Joly, Henri L. *Legend in Japanese Art* Bodley Head, London, 1908.

Keyes, Roger *The Male Journey in Japanese Prints* University of California, 1989.

Kôbe, Saza'emon 'Seishū Heiran-ki' in the series *Kaitei shiseki shūran* Vol. 25; Tokyo, 1902.

Kondo, Eiko, 'Inaka Genji series' in *Essays on Japanese Art Presented to Jack Hillier* M. Forrer (ed.), New York, 1982.

Kurita, Tadachika *Kaisei Mikawa Go-Fudo-ki* Tokyo, 1976.

Machiavelli, Niccoló *The Prince* translated with an introduction by George Bull, London 1961.

McCullough, Helen *The Taiheiki, A Chronicle of Medieval Japan* Columbia University Press, New York, 1959.

Masuda, Koh (ed.) *Kenkyūsha's New Japanese – English Dictionary* (4th edn.) Tokyo, 1974.

Miura, Jōshin 'Hōjō Godai-ki' in *Sengoku Shiryō Sōshō* 2nd Series, Vol. 1; Tokyo, 1965–67.

Momochi, Orinosuke, *Kōsei Iran-ki* Ueno, 1897.

Morris, Ivan *The Nobility of Failure, Tragic Heroes in the History of Japan* London, 1975.

Mosher, G. *Kyoto, A Contemplative Guide* Rutland, Vermont, 1964.

Murdoch, James *A History of Japan* Vol. I (2nd impression); London, 1925.

Needham, Joseph *A History of Science and Civilisation in China* Vol 5; London, 1975.

Nish, Ian 'A spy in Manchuria: Ishimitsu Makiyo' *Proceedings of the British Association for Japanese Studies* 1985.

Nish, Ian 'Japanese military intelligence on the eve of the Manchurian crisis' *Proceedings of the British Association for Japanese Studies*, 1986.

Okuno, Takahiro *Oda Nobunaga monjō no kenkyū* Tokyo, 1969.

Onoda, Hiroo *No Surrender – My Thirty-Year War* translated by Charles S. Terry, London, 1975.

Ota, Gyūichi *Shinchōkō-ki* Kuwata Tadachika (ed.), Tokyo, 1965.

Oze, Hoan, *Taikō-ki* Yoshida Yutaka (ed.), Tokyo, 1979.

Papinot, E. *Historical and Geographical Dictionary of Japan* Rutland, Vermont, 1972.

Rabinovitch, Judith N. *Shōmonki, the story of Masakado's rebellion* Tokyo, 1986.

Robinson, B.W. *Kuniyoshi, the Warrior Prints* London, 1982.

Rotermund, H.O. *Die Yamabushi* Hamburg, 1968.

Sadler, A.L. 'Heike Monogatari', *Transactions of the Asiatic Society of Japan* Vol. 46 and 49; Yokohama, 1918, 1921.

Sadler, A.L. *The Maker of Modern Japan* London, 1937.

Sanford, J.H. 'Shakuhachi Zen' *Monumenta Nipponica* Vol. 36, No. 1.

Sansom, G.B. *A History of Japan 1334–1615* London, 1961.

Saotome, Mitsugo *Ninja no sato ni shisu Rekishi Dokuhon* May 1965.

Sasama, Yoshihiko *Buke Senjin Sahō Shūsei* Tokyo, 1968.

Saunders, E. Dale *Mudrā. A study of symbolic gestures in Japanese Buddhist sculptures* Princeton, New Jersey, 1960.

Segi, Shinichi *Yoshitoshi, the splendid decadent* Tokyo, 1985.

Sugawara, Makoto *Lives of Master Swordsmen* Tokyo, 1985.

Sugiura, M. *Uesugi Kenshin no shi-in Kenkō Kyōshitsu*, April 1969.

Sugiyama, Hiroshi *Nihon no Rekishi* 11 *Sengoku daimyō* Tokyo, 1971.

Sun Tzu *The Art of War* translated and with an introduction by Samuel B. Griffith (with a Foreword by B.H. Liddell Hart); Oxford, 1963; New York, 1987.

Swanson, Paul 'Shūgendō and the Yoshino-Kumano Pilgrimage' *Monumenta Nipponica*, Vol. 36, No. 1.

Takahashi, Ken'ichi *Hata sashimono* Tokyo, 1965.

Takenouchi, Kakusai *Ehon Taikō-ki* Osaka, 1802.

Tanehiko, Ryūtei *Nise Murasaki Inaka Genji* in the series *Nihon Meicho Zenshū* Vols. 20 and 21; Tokyo, 1927.

Tanekiyo, Ryūsuitei *Yehon Toyotomi Kunki* Edo, 1857.

Tinios, Ellis *Kunisada* London, 1990.

Tokutomi, Iichiro *Oda-shi jidai* Tokyo, 1937.

Turnbull, Stephen *The Samurai – A Military History* London, 1977, 1988.

Turnbull, Stephen *Samurai Armies 1550–1615* London, 1979.

Turnbull, Stephen *Warlords of Japan* London, 1979.

Turnbull, Stephen *The Book of the Samurai* London, 1982.

Turnbull, Stephen *Samurai Warriors* London, 1987.

Turnbull, Stephen *Battles of the Samurai* London, 1987.

Turnbull, Stephen *Samurai Warlords – The Book of the Daimyō* London, 1989.

Turnbull, Stephen *The Lone Samurai and the Martial Arts* London, 1990.

Umezu, Jirō *Emakimono Sōshi* Kyoto, 1972.

Wakita, Osamu *Oda seiken ni kiso kōzō* Tokyo, 1977.

Watanabe, 'Keiichi *Kenshin no nana fushigi*' *Rekishi Dokuhon* September 1969.

Watatani, Kiyoshi *Nihon kengō hyakusen* Tokyo, 1971.

Watatani, Kiyoshi *Bugei ryūha hyakusen* Tokyo, 1972.

Wilson, William R. 'The Way of the Bow and Arrow. The Japanese Warrior in Konjaku Monogatari' *Monumenta Nipponica* Vol. 28, No. 2.

Yamada, Jirōkichi *Nihon Kendō-shi* Tokyo, 1960.

Yamada, Nakaba *Ghenkō, The Mongol Invasion of Japan* London, 1916.

Yamaguchi, S. *Ninja no seikatsu* Tokyo, 1969.

Yamamoto, Shigeki *Iga-Ueno jō* Ueno, 1976.

Yoshida, Yukata (ed.) *Taikō-ki* Tokyo, 1979.

Yūki, Shinichirō 'Koga jōkaku gun' *Rekishi Dokuhon* August 1988.

INDEX

Page numbers in *italic* refer to text illustrations; numbers in **bold** are those of the colour plates.

160